Learning

CHRIS AND JAMIE BAILEY

How to

A Devotional of Prayers and Practices
to Release Negative Emotions
and Achieve True Forgiveness

Forgive

Zeitgeist · New York

This publication contains the opinions and ideas of its author. It is intended to provide helpful and informative material on the subject matter covered. It is sold with the understanding that the author and publisher are not engaged in rendering professional services in the book. If the reader requires personal assistance or advice, a competent professional should be consulted. The author and publisher specifically disclaim any responsibility for any liability, loss, or risk, personal or otherwise, which is incurred as a consequence, directly or indirectly, of the use and application of any of the contents of this book.

Art © Getty Images/Pobytov
Book design John Calmeyer
Edited by Caroline Lee

Printed in the United States of America
1st Printing

This book is dedicated to its reader,

the one who, despite their hurt and pain,

is bravely choosing to follow Jesus

in forgiveness.

CONTENTS

INTRODUCTION

Forgiveness isn't just a one-time decision. It's a journey; one none of us asks to go on. It involves pain, grief, fear, and vulnerability. Much like grief and love, forgiveness and pain walk hand in hand. They are unlikely companions that always come together. If you have been hurt by someone and are finding yourself constantly replaying the offense in your mind, or if you feel stuck with anger, frustration, or sadness, then forgiveness may be the answer you need. By picking up this book, you are taking a very brave step. Most of us rarely want to do the hard stuff that require bravery, but we can trust that they're good when God calls us to them.

As Christian counselors, we have seen the challenging process of forgiveness unfold before our eyes on numerous occasions, and we have not been immune to this process ourselves. We have also witnessed the beauty that comes from the ashes of injury and hurt. We've seen and experienced enough pain and redemption firsthand to assure you that God dwells and rejoices in a forgiving heart.

Whether you're grappling with whether or not you will forgive, wrestling with the seeming injustice of forgiving an undeserving person, or ready for the freedom that comes with offering forgiveness, God will meet you where you are. His Word provides all the comfort and truth you need to get through this journey, and with him holding your hand in the process, you can trust that you will find healing. After all, if there's any message that Jesus wants to share with us, it's the incredible gift of forgiveness. The gift he came down from heaven to offer us in his grace is so beautifully manifested through his life, death, and resurrection.

Forgive, Forgiving, Forgiven

When betrayal, rejection, or offensively painful transgressions enter your life, it might be hard to imagine forgiving someone. You might be left wondering if you can ever get over the pain and damage that it has caused. Though it may not feel possible right now, yes, you can recover. The hope of healing is always possible, and forgiveness is often a vehicle God uses to get there.

Sometimes, when others have wounded us, we end up feeling shame and guilt. It may seem like something is wrong with you because you're struggling to forgive. You may also believe you're disappointing God because you still feel anger toward the person you're trying to forgive, no matter how hard you try not to. While this process of forgiveness is challenging, there is good news. Ultimately, unforgiveness is a choice. It's a matter of being unwilling to forgive and holding on to anger, resentment, and the feeling of being owed something. But since you are holding this book, you've already made a big step in the right direction toward developing a forgiving heart.

The Reality of Forgiveness

When we look to Scripture, we find the power of forgiveness at its very center. The great lengths Jesus went to by dying on the cross, clearly shows us that forgiveness is something God deems essential. In Matthew 26:39, we see Jesus preparing to face his death on the cross. As the time drew near, we see a glimpse into the significant cost Jesus would pay when he asked the Father to take away this "cup of suffering." This forgiveness would be costly for Jesus, but he still chose to offer it to us in his great love, even though we didn't deserve it. Offering forgiveness is about grasping the bigger picture of love despite its sometimes painful cost. As you face the challenge of forgiving, take comfort in knowing that forgiveness was hard for Jesus, too.

One of the biggest challenges of forgiveness is the desire for it to be earned. If we follow the example of Jesus, we see that although we didn't deserve forgiveness, he still chose to forgive. We did nothing to earn his forgiveness as he hung on the cross, yet he offered it through his grace. When offenders proclaim true repentance, they do not take forgiveness for granted.

We also see in Scripture the same people repeating patterns of sinning and seeking forgiveness repeatedly. However, forgiveness is not about being permissive or emboldening people to keep sinning or causing pain in others, even though some still choose to do so. When this repeated sinning is the case, forgiveness becomes something that grants you freedom to move forward and away from them.

Ultimately, God calls us to forgive in all circumstances, earned or not, because forgiveness is about following Jesus and bringing glory to his name. Forgiveness is an opportunity to remember that, as followers of Jesus, we can do the unimaginable when we rely on his help. In our darkest moments, we can follow his example and trust that we don't have to do it alone. It can be a process that sometimes comes easy; other times, it takes everything you have to move forward while you wait for painful emotions to subside. Regardless of where you are on this journey, God has a way forward for you.

Jesus' Forgiveness

Our desire for you is that every nook and cranny of your heart will be filled with peace and brimming with God's goodness to fuel you forward. You will discover so much on your journey of forgiveness. You will see God's heart and the beauty of Jesus' forgiveness. You will learn to care for the struggle of being hurt. The journey leads to a peace and joy only the Lord can give, even if you don't receive reconciliation or the outcome you hoped for.

God is always near to the brokenhearted, and he longs to walk this path with you. He plans to bring purpose to your pain and draw you closer to him as you experience comfort and healing.

Reflecting on our own lives, we are reminded how much God has been there for us as individuals and as a couple. Both of us spent years living in bitterness and resentment. Jamie put up walls; Chris became a people pleaser. We both vowed never to be hurt again, but ultimately, we were the ones that were held captive and hurt.

It wasn't until we each surrendered our lives to Christ that we experienced the value of forgiveness. In God's grace, he opened our eyes and hearts to see that forgiving, even to those that don't deserve it, wasn't about our offenders or us. It was about him. But also, in his grace, we found freedom in our new, forgiving hearts.

We pray that this devotional will bring you the sweet freedom and truth that speaks to your soul and unleashes the transformative power of God's Word in your life.

How to Use This Book

The key features of this devotional will provide you with support, understanding, and guidance on your forgiveness journey. Through this book, you'll deepen your understanding of forgiveness and examine how to forgive.

It is divided into two parts, one with support and encouragement and the other with practical application. In part one, 52 weekly devotionals are designed to root you in Scripture and encourage you with truth. You will learn about forgiveness and find relatable stories and testimonies of others who have also walked this faith journey. There will be Scriptures to reflect on and structured prayers you can take with you throughout your day.

In part two, you will find 25 exercises and practical tools, many of which we use in our counseling practice, that are flexible enough to use with multiple devotions. On each day of devotion, you will be directed to the specific exercise that applies to it. These exercises are meant to draw you closer to the Lord so you can walk peacefully throughout each day. Your only job will be to sit down with an open heart and be ready to express your struggles and desires openly and honestly with the Lord. Expect God to meet you.

This devotional is meant to offer you a place of healing. Use it as a guide to find relief on this journey of forgiveness as you process, accept, and heal. He's with you every step of the way.

PART I

THE DEVOTIONS

God Will Help You Forgive

Do not be afraid or discouraged, for the Lord will
personally go ahead of you. He will be with you; He
will neither fail you nor abandon you.

DEUTERONOMY 31:8

Do you sometimes wonder if you'll ever be able to forgive
those who have hurt you? Does it feel like an impossible task? God
understands that. He knows this is a big ask of you and doesn't expect
you to go on this forgiveness journey alone.

God promises to be with us whenever we face a trial or hard times.
In Deuteronomy, the Lord had just asked the Israelites to journey into
the Promised Land. While that sounds good on paper, the reality for
them was that the Promised Land contained giants and many people
who could, by all accounts, kill them. It was a big ask of God and a
scary journey ahead.

In response to their fear and discouragement, God graciously
reminded them that they would not be alone. Not only would he be
going with them, but he would also go ahead of them. This promise
was not just for the Israelites. It's also a promise for you. God is in the
wilderness of unforgiveness with you, and he has already journeyed
ahead, knowing the goodness of the land of forgiveness that lies there.

You are not alone. Instead, trust that God will never send you to a place where you aren't meant to go, and he certainly won't ever send you alone.

For Relief and Peace

Exploring Forgiveness (page 154) God is always ready to help you. The problem is knowing where you need his help. This week you will uncover your beliefs about forgiveness and why it sometimes might be more difficult for you. As you explore your thoughts and feelings, seek the Lord's guidance to overcome any obstacles that he reveals.

Dear Lord, Even though I am scared of this process, and it is difficult to do, I will trust you, knowing you have in mind what's good for me. In Jesus' name. Amen.

What Exactly Is Forgiveness?

Jesus said, "This is how you should pray:

"Father, may your name be kept holy. May your

Kingdom come soon. Give us each day the food

we need, and forgive us our sins, as we forgive

those who sin against us."

LUKE 11:2–4

In the book of Luke, the disciples had a request for Jesus. They knew other rabbis were teaching their disciples how to pray, so they asked Jesus to teach them as well. Jesus instructed to first recognize God's holiness, ask for their daily needs, and then seek forgiveness, just as they forgave others. Since God calls us to pray continuously, the request to "forgive us our sins, as we forgive those who sin against us" illustrates that forgiveness should be a daily way of life for the believer.

Forgiveness is a decision. It's a choice someone makes to follow God in obedience. Jesus offered no caveat about what transgressions deserved forgiveness and which didn't. Instead, he says to choose it daily, even before you repent of your sins to the Father.

Since God asks us to make forgiveness a daily decision, let's look at what forgiveness is:

- an offer to pardon an offender,
- releasing any resentment,
- giving up your right for revenge,
- granting them full relief from paying their debt to you.

Wow, that is a tall order, yet God says to do it daily. It's okay if this seems overwhelming and you struggle to forgive. The good news is that God knows how difficult forgiveness is—that's why we should do it every day because once is usually not enough to alleviate our hearts.

For Relief and Peace

Wake Up Your Self-Worth (page 161) You must first root your identity as God's precious child before you obediently follow him and receive his best for your life. When you understand the value the Lord has given you and all he has done for you, following him, especially in the harder things like forgiveness, will be something you *want* to do. Understanding who God is and how much he loves you will make your desire to please him grow stronger.

Dear Lord, You are holy and deserve all the praise. Thank you for meeting my daily needs. Please forgive me as I learn to offer others the same kind of forgiveness. In Jesus' name. Amen.

Why We Need Forgiveness

But God showed his great love for us by

sending Christ to die for us while we were still

sinners. And since we have been made right in

God's sight by the blood of Christ, he will certainly

save us from God's condemnation.

ROMANS 5:8–9

It's estimated that about 92 percent of people struggle with perfectionism. Those perfectionistic tendencies can easily carry over to our relationship with God. We—Chris and Jamie—are both prone to it. Before we knew Jesus, we believed we had to clean up for him—that we needed to get our lives together first, and then we could turn to him.

If we look to Scripture, we will find the exact opposite. God says he is right there for us amid our sin. While we are seeking to make ourselves look better than others by gossiping, judging, or any other self-gratifying act, God is right there waiting for us. Even in our sin, he wants us to seek reconnection through repentance with him. Our sins, our wrongdoings, are exactly why he sent his Son to die. He became the remedy for our sins. If we never acknowledge our imperfections, including our sins, we will never realize we need Jesus.

We cannot be connected to the Father without his forgiveness. Your sins plus his grace and forgiveness equal a restored relationship. That's the ultimate beauty of forgiveness: it doesn't require perfection to receive it abundantly.

For Relief and Peace

God's Truth (page 139) God is holy and without sin, unlike us. When we've been hurt by someone, we tend to forget this. When we gaze upon their glaring sin, it can be difficult to admit we have our own sin that was once forgiven. God's gift of forgiveness reminds us that we can give it, too.

In this week's exercise, instead of comparing yourself to the one who wronged you, you will see yourself compared to a perfect, loving God. When you are reminded of the many attributes of God, it will be easier to reflect on your own need for forgiveness, which will ultimately lead to godly humility and healing.

Dear Lord, Thank you for desiring a relationship with me even when I am undeserving and fall short. Open my heart to receive your full grace today. In Jesus' name. Amen.

What the Bible Says about Forgiveness

And forgive us our sins, as we have forgiven those

who sin against us.

MATTHEW 6:12

Even when God's Word addresses forgiveness extensively, it can feel like a disconnect when we try to apply it in our lives. As Christian counselors who deal with this topic frequently, we think forgiveness is covered so much in the Bible because God knows it's hard—but it's also important.

We can find freedom in forgiveness. Forgiveness from God removes our need to pay the debt of our sin, which means that it also removes the need for our transgressors to repay us. That second part is the hard part to grasp.

Kimberly lost her son, who was tragically hit by a drunk driver while walking home from school. This tragedy could have consumed her whole life in multiple ways. The stewing anger for this negligent, intoxicated man could have caused her as much pain as the grief over the loss of her son.

But Kimberly, in all the humility and full recognition of God's forgiveness for her, chose to forgive this man just as God had forgiven her. She didn't minimize the devastating pain he caused or the injustice of it all. So, as she poured her heart out to God, she realized there could never be a compensation high enough for her son's life. She knew she had to rely on God's strength to get through the pain of losing her son, a pain she knew he understood.

For Relief and Peace

Visualizing God's Justice (page 148) Forgiveness can come at a high price, especially when justice isn't served or the pain of the wrongdoing is one that lasts a lifetime. This week's exercise reminds you that you are not left alone in your pain. As your loving Father, God is always doing work on your behalf.

Dear Lord, I am so grateful for your forgiveness to me and though it is hard to give to others, help me to have a forgiving heart like yours. In Jesus' name. Amen.

What Forgiveness Is Not

Guard your heart above all else,

for it determines the course of your life.

PROVERBS 4:23

It's common within the Christian community to take the definition of forgiveness and add a few things to it. While the intentions are often good and meant to help with godliness, these unnecessary additions can become harmful and take us away from understanding what forgiveness really is about.

Forgiveness does not mean that what happened is okay. You can forgive and put up a boundary. Telling someone what is okay for you and setting boundaries is separate from forgiving them. Forgiveness does not mean tolerating harmful things. It also doesn't mean that the person gets let off the hook. Throughout Scripture, we find examples of people suffering the consequences of their choices and these consequences reveal to them ways to learn and grow. But withholding forgiveness doesn't help you or the offender. It is also not our responsibility to impose consequences onto others because we want to teach them a lesson or seek retaliation.

Forgiveness also doesn't mean you must hide your feelings and move on. Forgiveness is a healing journey, not always a healed destination. You don't have to forgive, forget, and move on as if nothing happened. Ultimately, it's up to you to determine what you will allow to enter your heart and do your best to protect it from toxic behaviors and relationships where your boundaries are not respected. Forgiveness doesn't negate that.

For Relief and Peace

Evaluating Healthy Boundaries (page 165) Your relationships are only as healthy as your boundaries are. In this week's exercise, learn about the value of having boundaries in your relationships. Applying boundaries will ensure your relationships will be emotionally and mentally sound, safe, and thriving.

- -

Dear Lord, My heart is heavy, and I am feeling consumed by the pain that I am experiencing. Please help me protect my heart and emotional well-being. In Jesus' name. Amen.

- -

To Forgive or Not to Forgive

Get rid of all bitterness, rage, anger, harsh words,

and slander, as well as all types of evil behavior.

Instead, be kind to each other, tenderhearted,

forgiving one another, just as God through Christ

has forgiven you.

EPHESIANS 4:31–32

In Ephesians 4, Paul provides the believer with some instructions. He's also laying out some choices by saying that we can choose bitterness, rage, anger, harsh words, slander, and evilness, or we can choose to be kind, tenderhearted, forgiving, and ultimately be more like Christ, who has forgiven us.

There's a clear right answer; but the struggle is that the first list comes naturally—we must dig deeper for that second list. The two contradicting lists also reveal that if you don't choose one, you're choosing the other. If we aren't tenderhearted, we're harsh. If we're not kind, we're prone to slander. We experience bitterness, anger, and potentially rage if we choose not to forgive.

It's important to position ourselves close to God to do the difficult things he desires of us. We must humble ourselves and allow the Holy Spirit to lead us to become more tenderhearted. Not only should we pray and seek God's wisdom, but also practice being still in his presence so we can hear his voice as he guides us.

To rid ourselves of rage and bitterness, we must become very intentional about not stewing on the wrongs committed. When we become bitter over the offenses, it easily leads to rage and anger. When we allow anger to take root, it will often come out of our mouths in harsh words and slander. Yet when we focus on how kind God has been to us, it becomes much easier to be tenderhearted and extend kindness to others.

Instead of treating these contradictory verses as a long list of commands, you might find it easier to start with what God says is best—kindness—and the rest of what he desires will flow more naturally.

For Relief and Peace

Motivation Chart (page 152) In this week's exercise, evaluate different scenarios to see where the decision to forgive or not, could potentially lead.

Dear Lord, Thank you for speaking the truth and directing me to make good choices in my life. Give me the wisdom to choose wisely today. In Jesus' name. Amen.

WEEK 7

Should I Forgive and Forget?

I—yes, I alone—will blot out your sins for my own sake and will never think of them again.

ISAIAH 43:25

We often hear "forgive and forget" when we can't let go of certain past hurts—it can feel callous and uncaring. So, we must first ask, "Is this concept even biblical?" The answer is no. Nowhere in Scripture does God call on us to forget when we have been wronged. He is the only one who does that. He calls us to let go of bitterness, anger, and malice, but he doesn't ever tell us to forget the offense.

While we're not meant to stew on the wrongs done to us, we also don't want to be weighed down by painful memories. While we likely can't forget the wrongdoing and the pain, we can move on from it.

Our brains were not designed to hold on to every memory. Forgetfulness can sometimes naturally come with the passage of time or our hearts can expand in ways we didn't expect. But there are also traumatic events that you can't forget, but instead force you to remember them constantly. If you're struggling to move on because your mind is consumed with the memory, consider finding wise counsel—such as a therapist who specializes in trauma—to help build a realistic path away from those memories and harmful thought cycles. There is no shame in seeking help. You deserve healing.

For Relief and Peace

How to Stop Ruminating (page 167) Whenever something is weighing heavily upon your heart, it's important to limit how much space and time it takes up in your mind. If you ruminate too long on negativity or stress, it can spiral into negative thought patterns, leading to even more stress and worry. In this week's exercise, slow down negative thought cycles and make room to seek and focus on God's truth.

Dear Lord, Lead my focus away from the wrongs that have been done to me. Please direct my path so I can move forward. In Jesus' name. Amen.

Forgiveness Is a Process

No, dear brothers and sisters, I have not achieved

it, but I focus on this one thing: Forgetting the past

and looking forward to what lies ahead, I press on

to reach the end of the race and receive the

heavenly prize for which God, through Christ Jesus,

is calling us.

PHILIPPIANS 3:13–14

Perhaps you've decided to forgive and yet still struggle with all the feelings, and even some bitterness, toward that person. Forgiving someone can feel unnatural to our instinctual inclination to protect ourselves. But as difficult as it is to forgive, you are making the choice to be obedient to God.

Forgiveness is like a muscle that needs to be worked out and strengthened rather than a destination. Just like Paul shares in Philippians, you're on a journey to forget what's behind you and press on to the goal of Christlikeness.

Forgiveness only needs to be offered once but implementing it takes time. Let this journey be between you and God. He is there to help you, and there is no pressure to reach the finish line today. One step forward at a time is enough; little by little, you'll get there.

30   LEARNING HOW TO FORGIVE

For Relief and Peace

Steps to Asking for Forgiveness (page 156) This week, continue the process of forgiveness by focusing on tangible steps. This exercise provides the grace you need to allow forgiveness to unfold little by little or to start anew.

Dear Lord, Give me the strength I need to keep moving forward. I choose to forgive and need your help to finish this process. In Jesus' name. Amen.

Forgiveness Is About You

A time to search and a time to quit searching. A
time to keep and a time to throw away.

ECCLESIASTES 3:6

King Solomon, the author of Ecclesiastes, was known for his
great wisdom. As a king of great wealth, he had anything he wanted at
his fingertips, only to find it all meaningless. His search for wealth and
fame resulted in emptiness, and he warns us not to do the same. What
truly matters in life is not the things of this world; it's people. It's a life
lived well for the glory of God.

Solomon says there is a time to quit searching and let go. That
means when things are beyond your control, like someone causing you
pain or harm, there comes a point where you must release it and move
on. This letting go is not for the offender. It's for you. Continuing to
search for answers and keeping the offense close can drag you down.
It makes your life harder. Learning to let go is about making your life
lighter by choosing not to carry the weight someone else has given
you. Carrying the burden of unforgiveness was never meant to be part
of your identity.

Forgiveness is the freedom to refuse carrying other peoples' sins
and burdens. Despite all the pain, he has a greater purpose for you
that is unfolding. Drop the heavy bags of unforgiveness so that you
can move more freely through life.

For Relief and Peace

Letter to Self (page 141) As you put pen to paper in this week's exercise, explore why things happened as they did or are the way they are. More likely, you will find that there is no reason for either. Relieve yourself from the responsibility of feeling like you had any control over the situation. Doing so will help you let go of the burden you are carrying, and you can move forward more easily.

Dear Lord, Thank you for the wisdom I need to walk in freedom. Help me let go and move forward. In Jesus' name. Amen.

Benefits of Forgiveness

A cheerful heart is good medicine, but a broken

spirit saps a person's strength.

PROVERBS 17:22

There's not much that breaks a spirit quite like holding a grudge. It may seem as if it's easier to remain in unforgiveness, but in truth, it requires greater effort. Resentments are like heavy weights shackled to your feet that you drag around wherever you go. The truth is that when you hold on to pain, you end up paying a high price. The one who has hurt you walks around freely while you are left to face the heavy burdens of the harm they caused every day. When you relinquish the grudge through forgiveness, you exchange bitterness and pain for peace and hope.

Forgiveness comes with some very real benefits. When you don't need to put your energy into carrying around a broken spirit, your body can use those resources for what it was designed for—keeping you healthy. Your body will regulate itself, and that results in lower blood pressure, a stronger immune system, and improved heart health.

Forgiveness not only impacts your own health, but it bleeds into other parts of your life, such as an increase in the quality of your relationships. Your lifted spirits can be a light into people around you. Think of a time when you've been with someone who was holding a grudge. Maybe it's over their ex or a boss they're upset with. Are they draining you or life-giving? Though not intentional, what is in our hearts is what comes out of our mouths, and grudges affect our attitudes and our conversations.

When you walk in forgiveness, you protect your health, happiness, and relationships.

For Relief and Peace

Filling Your Joy Bucket (page 145) Choosing joy can help redirect your heart's focus. In this week's exercise, explore ways to experience joy daily. Uncover the benefits of joy found in Scripture to help carry you in your walk through forgiveness.

....

Dear Lord, I want to be physically and emotionally healthy. I give you my grudges today so my body can thrive. In Jesus' name. Amen.

....

Remembering the Gift of Forgiveness

He is so rich in kindness and grace that he

purchased our freedom with the blood of his Son

and forgave our sins.

EPHESIANS 1:7

If you've been hurt in significant and painful ways, you may cringe or physically recoil as you think about how undeserving or unforgivable that person is. Maybe a slew of minor transgressions has happened to you over the years. The idea of forgiveness brings up the past, and you can still feel a bit of a sting from those experiences.

It's easy to think of the pain inflicted on us, but we should also remember that we've all needed forgiveness from Jesus. The reality is that we are both of those people: the ones who need forgiveness and the ones who must give it.

Forgiveness is an incredible gift; it's given to us to offer, in turn, to others. It requires sacrifice, but it is also a gift rich in kindness and grace. God gave us such a sacrificial display of forgiveness when he sent his Son to the cross to restore our relationship with him. Can you imagine for a moment what your life would be like without Christ's forgiveness? Oh, the shame, guilt, and hopelessness we would carry.

When we realize how much we needed forgiveness in the past and will need it again in the future, it makes forgiving others with grace and kindness much easier.

For Relief and Peace

Gratitude List (page 132) This week's exercise has three different components. Each one will help you remember all you have and all that is good. Whatever you focus on, you will magnify it. Spend time being grateful as you shift your focus from pain to the goodness of God.

Dear Lord, Thank you for the gift of your Son when I was once separated from you and in need of forgiveness. Remind me that I have received this costly gift from you. In Jesus' name. Amen.

Seeking Forgiveness

Confess your sins to each other and pray for each

other so that you may be healed. The earnest prayer

of a righteous person has great power and

produces wonderful results.

JAMES 5:16

There are two parts to forgiveness: the one who offers forgiveness and the one who needs forgiveness. Sometimes, seeking forgiveness involves a simple apology, and other times, it may require making amends as well. Let's say you said you would be home in enough time to go out to dinner with your spouse, but you got involved in a project at work and lost track of time. In this case, offering an apology may be sufficient. However, if this is the third time you've made a promise and left your spouse waiting or disappointed, you will likely need to make amends. This may mean you plan a special night out or become intentional about showing up on time from now on.

Confessing your wrongdoings and taking ownership of them is an important part of seeking forgiveness. It's not enough to just be sorry. You must confess that you are sorry. Seeking forgiveness is relational, and God calls you to involve the person you hurt. By confessing your sin, you show that you understand your actions were hurtful.

For Relief and Peace

Steps to Asking for Forgiveness (page 156) Good apologies have specific attributes that make them good. If any of these attributes are missing, the apology may not be received as authentic. In the exercise for the week, we lay out these attributes into helpful steps that you can go through in advance anytime you need to right a wrong or give a heartfelt apology.

Dear Lord, I want to be quick to apologize when I am wrong. Fill me with humility and help me confess my sins freely. In Jesus' name. Amen.

Seeking God's Forgiveness

When the cool evening breezes were blowing, the
man and his wife heard the Lord God walking about
in the garden. So they hid from the Lord God
among the trees. Then the Lord God called to the
man, "Where are you?"

GENESIS 3:8–9

Returning to the Garden of Eden, where the first sin was
committed, we find Adam and Eve hiding in shame. They knew they
had just disobeyed God, and their first response was to fear him
instead of run to him. They hid in their shame instead of seeking his
forgiveness. Clearly this shameful response didn't die with Adam
and Eve.

There can be a lot of guilt and shame when we sin, but that
shouldn't keep us from God. It should propel us toward him. When
Adam and Eve sinned in the garden, God's response was to seek them
out. He knew they had sinned, and even with that knowledge, God
went to them. The God who sought them in their shame in the garden
is the same God we have today. Even in our sin, he wants a relationship.
Our shame and sin can drive a wedge between God and us. It takes a

conscious effort to fight through that shame—once we bring our shame to light, it disappears. God is waiting for us there.

God is compassionate. He is the remedy for our sins and our shame. He is the last one we should feel shame in front of. God knew Adam and Eve were ashamed of their nakedness, so he provided clothes for them. Still, today, when we bring our shame to God, he provides.

For Relief and Peace

Steps to Asking for Forgiveness (page 156) There will be many times in life when you will need to repent and seek God's forgiveness. Perhaps you need a right relationship restored with him because you gave into your flesh instead of being obedient. Or maybe you have never entered into a saving relationship with God through Jesus.

Through this week's exercise, examine salvation and the repentance of sin by going through the practical steps to seek forgiveness from God and others.

Dear Lord, Forgive me for doubting you. Forgive me for the times I've run in shame. Thank you for always providing for me. In Jesus' name.

Amen.

Forgiving Myself

Finally, I confessed all my sins to you and stopped

trying to hide my guilt. I said to myself, "I will

confess my rebellion to the Lord." And you forgave

me! All my guilt is gone.

PSALM 32:5

Guilt, self-loathing, harsh judgment, and lofty expectations are all clues that you may struggle with forgiving yourself. If you're anything like me, Jamie, you probably have extremely high standards for yourself. I've struggled with forgiving myself for decisions I made, for not being good enough, for not trying harder, the list goes on and on. Nothing I ever did felt good enough; when it didn't, I would beat myself up over not being better.

I had no problem offering grace and compassion to others, but when it came to extending it to myself, that was off the table. I was beyond forgiveness. I knew better, yet I kept struggling and repeating the same harmful patterns of negative self-talk and self-accusation. No mercy, no grace, no forgiveness, just ridicule was all I felt I deserved.

When I choose not to forgive myself, I don't believe what God says. In a search to "feel" forgiven, I miss that "I am" forgiven. When God says he forgives you and your guilt is gone, your guilt needs to *be* gone, despite how guilty you still feel. When those negative, accusatory words arise, release them to God and ask him to fill your mind with truth. Know that just because you are still feeling guilty it doesn't mean that you are. Your feelings do not get to have authority over God's Word.

For Relief and Peace

Letter to Self (page 141) This week, select a prompt to write a letter to yourself and practice giving yourself grace. It can often be easier to offer grace to someone who has wronged you, even in a deeply painful way, than it is to give it to yourself. As you write and slow down your thinking, make room for the Holy Spirit to move your heart.

Dear Lord, Forgive me of all my sins and help me

not to act as if your forgiveness is meaningless.

In Jesus' name. Amen.

Why Is Forgiveness So Difficult?

Then Jesus said, "Come to me, all of you who are weary and carry heavy burdens, and I will give you rest. Take my yoke upon you. Let me teach you, because I am humble and gentle at heart, and you will find rest for your souls."

MATTHEW 11:28–29

Mary was 83 when she passed away after almost a lifetime of suffering. She lost two of her three children to a genetic disease. She also suffered from a lifetime of never forgiving God for what she believed he had done to her. Forgiveness for Mary was just too difficult.

There is so much compassion to be found for a woman like Mary, who carried such a magnitude of pain. But there is also a great sadness for her, because she never found her way to forgiveness. Unforgiveness doesn't just happen to people; it is often something they've been taught or used to protect themselves.

Some people have never witnessed the act of forgiveness and only had judgment and blame modeled for them. Others feel safer and more powerful by holding on to the grudge. Some have never received forgiveness for themselves and, therefore, struggle to offer it to others.

When forgiveness feels difficult, as it did for Mary, that is the best time to give the Lord your heavy burdens and allow him to provide you rest. He is calling you near, let him teach you with his love.

For Relief and Peace

Removing Barriers to Forgiveness (page 122) In this exercise, discover potential barriers that make forgiveness difficult. By exploring specific barriers and identifying the ones blocking you, you can take your exact struggles to the Lord.

Dear Lord, Take my burdens in exchange for your rest. Soften my heart and teach me your ways. In Jesus' name. Amen.

Forgiving Without an Apology

But when you are praying, first forgive anyone you are holding a grudge against, so that your Father in heaven will forgive your sins, too.

MARK 11:25

Shannon had gone through a difficult divorce, but co-parenting with her ex-husband was proving to be even more difficult. He was hard enough to be married to, but it was just as hard not to be married to him because of how he was trying to turn their children against her. It seemed like she had more and more to forgive him for, and he wasn't the least bit sorry.

It can be very frustrating when someone has hurt you, and they don't seem to care. That lack of consideration will understandably make it easy for a grudge to grow. But what God says to do instead is to still forgive them. Forgiveness is so important to God that he wants you to release people from the snare of unforgiveness when you come to him in prayer.

This forgiveness is more of an attitude of your heart. He wants your soul cleansed from any unforgiveness when you come before him. Even though the matter may not be settled in your lifetime, his desire is for it to be settled in your heart. When Shannon focused on the Lord instead of on her ex, she was less provoked by what he was doing and more at peace with how the Lord began transforming her heart.

For Relief and Peace

Write and Rip (page 136) Letting go can be hard, especially if you've been robbed of an apology or an opportunity to share your feelings or from confronting the person who caused you pain. In this exercise, share your raw and unfiltered words and you will find a tangible way to let them go so you can begin to move on.

Dear Lord, It is not easy to forgive those who refuse to apologize. Change my heart to offer forgiveness despite their unwillingness to apologize. In Jesus' name. Amen.

When Forgiveness Feels Impossible

Now let your unfailing love comfort me, just as you

promised me, your servant.

PSALM 119:76

Corrie ten Boom, a Dutch Christian woman captured with her sister for hiding Jewish people during the Holocaust, had more to forgive than most ever will. They were sent to a concentration camp where they were humiliated, starved, and treated inhumanely. Her sister didn't survive.

Corrie survived to tell the stories that came from this torturous camp. During one such speaking event, after sharing her story, Corrie was approached by a man she immediately recognized. In her mind, his brown coat and hat turned instantly into a blue uniform with a recognizable skull and crossbones cap, the same uniform that took part in the death of her sister and her cruel suffering.

As this man, now a Christian, approached her, confessing his time as a guard in her camp, begging for forgiveness, she wasn't sure she could offer it. But at that moment, God gently spoke to her heart, and with fear and anger still present, she reached out her hand to meet his and offered forgiveness. She realized then that withholding her forgiveness would never erase the damage he had caused. She felt

God's comfort flood her heart as she grasped his hand and knew she made the right choice.

The comfort God provided Corrie as she forgave the unforgivable is offered to you in the same way. He will also provide for you when you doubt yourself and feel limited in your strength to forgive.

For Relief and Peace

Removing Barriers to Forgiveness (page 122) In this week's exercise, we will seek the Lord's strength for forgiving those who are harder to forgive.

Dear Lord, Soften my heart and help me put my full trust in your comfort. In Jesus' name. Amen.

Unforgiveness Gives the Enemy Power

And "don't sin by letting anger control you." Don't

let the sun go down while you are still angry, for

anger gives a foothold to the devil.

EPHESIANS 4:26–27

When we are in a state of unforgiveness, we hold onto festering anger—and it won't take long for it to morph into other undesirable emotions and ailments. According to Ephesians, stewing in anger opens the door for the enemy to work in your life. This doesn't mean you're not allowed to feel because feeling angry, especially when you've been wronged, is entirely normal. It means don't avoid dealing with your anger.

We shouldn't forget that our anger hurts ourselves way more than it does the person we are angry at. Anger that is not dealt with and is linked with unforgiveness becomes like a mind virus. The more we focus on it, the more it grows. The more you think about how you were wronged, the madder you get. All the while, the enemy sits back and applauds.

Anger and unforgiveness steal your peace. Your heart and mind won't be at rest if you're dealing with triggers and painful memories;

you'll be constantly on edge or get upset on a whim. Anger and unforgiveness demand that you always stay on guard to protect yourself against being injured again. The enemy loves this kind of exhausting self-destruction that comes from anger and unforgiveness. When you trust the Lord to protect you instead of staying vigilant on your own, you open your heart to forgiveness and take away opportunities for the enemy to work in your life. Is it time to remove the foothold he has been given?

For Relief and Peace

Victory Prayers (page 130) To conquer anger and any attempt the enemy takes to keep you from God's will, you will need to stand firm on the Word of God. This week, utilize powerful Scriptures to claim the truth, foster an attitude of forgiveness, and disrupt any schemes of the enemy.

Dear Lord, I don't want the enemy to have his way in my life. If I have any undealt with anger over the pain I've been caused, please make it clear to me so I can begin to deal with it. In Jesus' name. Amen.

The Dangers of Unforgiveness

Then the king called in the man he had forgiven
and said, 'You evil servant! I forgave you that
tremendous debt because you pleaded with me.
Shouldn't you have mercy on your fellow servant,
just as I had mercy on you?' Then the angry king
sent the man to prison to be tortured until he
had paid his entire debt.

MATTHEW 18:32–34

Matthew 18:21-35 tells the story of a king that forgave the large
debt of a servant who begged for mercy. Yet, that same servant went
out after receiving forgiveness and came across a fellow servant who
owed less to him than he initially owed the king. Unlike the king, he
demanded this debt to be repaid even though the man begged for
more time to repay him.

Instead of offering the same forgiveness that he was offered, he
had this man arrested until he repaid what he owed. When the king
heard what he did, he called the servant evil for not demonstrating to

his fellow servant the same mercy the king had shown him. As a result, the king threw this unforgiving man in jail, not only to pay his debt but also to be tortured. If unforgiveness is allowed to take root, it can cause us harm.

When we choose not to forgive others as Christ, our King, has forgiven us, we are also choosing a form of torture. It may not be physical torture in a jail cell, but the torture of living a life of bitterness and resentment. God wants you to live debt-free, but he also wants you to offer the same freedom to others.

For Relief and Peace

Finding Peace in Nature (page 124) This exercise will give you space and time to clear your head and calm your nervous system. Sit outside and bask quietly in creation or get your body moving while interacting with the Lord through prayer and active listening.

Dear Lord, Thank you for forgiving me of such a large debt. Help me to offer others the same forgiveness of their debts owed to me. In Jesus' name. Amen.

The Downside of Unforgiveness

If you forgive those who sin against you, your heavenly Father will forgive you. But if you refuse to forgive others, your Father will not forgive your sins.

MATTHEW 6:14–15

At first glance, Matthew 6 feels very weighty. It can seem like our salvation is at stake if we struggle to forgive others immediately, but this isn't the case. This is good news, but remember that it's still a big deal. If you refuse to forgive someone who's sinned against you, it *will* impact your fellowship with God.

It's as if you're throwing a wrench in your relationship with the Lord. Could you be close friends with someone who didn't care about things that were important to you? What if they never wanted to do something you felt was very significant? It would be difficult to be close to that person.

It's the same thing with our relationship with God. It's hard to be close when we're unwilling to do something he says is very important. Part of any healthy relationship is making what's important to our loved ones important to us. This is especially true in our relationship with God.

And if you've been hurt, especially deeply hurt, a close relationship with God will help you pave a path to expanding generosity to forgive others.

For Relief and Peace

Attributes of God (page 163) If you desire the best relationship with God, be curious to know more about him and get in his presence. Whenever you feel distant from him, it's a good time to open his Word and be reminded of his goodness. As you get in the Word and grow in your knowledge of him, the Holy Spirit will reveal to your heart how to trust him through this forgiveness process.

Dear Lord, You know all of my hurts, and I don't want anything to disrupt my relationship with you at a time when I need you the most. Help me to have your heart for forgiveness. In Jesus' name. Amen.

Being Scared to Forgive

So we can say with confidence, "The Lord is my
helper, so I will have no fear. What can mere people
do to me?"

HEBREWS 13:6

Crystal and James had a great relationship until one day
Crystal discovered James was having an inappropriate conversation
with a past girlfriend. She wondered what else he might be hiding, and
if she knew the whole truth. Her mind raced.

James confessed his wrongdoing and assured her it was just one
conversation. He felt ashamed for falling into temptation. James
immediately deleted this woman from all his social media accounts and
blocked her on his phone. He ensured Crystal had all his passwords
and was willing to be fully transparent. He apologized profusely, but
somehow, they struggled to move forward.

Crystal felt stuck, too. She wanted to believe James and even saw
proof that he was repentant. The problem for Crystal was fear. When
someone has hurt you, trusting them again requires vulnerability, and
they have the power to hurt you again. To get past this, you must allow
yourself to risk that pain again, especially if they have already begun to
build some trust. However, taking that risk is easier when your trust is
ultimately in God, knowing that he will be there for you no matter

what. Unlike people, he is always trustworthy and will never let you down.

Holding on to unforgiveness can make you feel safe, but it's a lie. Unforgiveness doesn't protect you from being hurt. People are always capable of causing us pain. God asks us to separate forgiveness from someone's ability to hurt you. He reminds us that he will always be there to help us, no matter what happens to us. Our trust in him is what allows us to set our fears aside and move forward.

For Relief and Peace

Gaining Hope and Confidence During Dark Times (page 137) When emotions are heavy, and fear is prevalent, there is nothing better than steadying yourself with the truth of God's Word. In this week's exercise, calm your mind and find comfort in remembering who God is and the safe place he can provide for you in times of fear.

Dear Lord, I am ready to let my fears go. Help me

to trust that you are my protector and helper.

In Jesus' name. Amen.

Unforgiveness: A False Sense of Safety

This High Priest of ours understands our

weaknesses, for he faced all of the same testings we

do, yet he did not sin.

HEBREWS 4:15

God created everyone to have the same needs. We all desire to be loved, to be significant, and to be safe. When those needs are threatened, we react and do whatever we need to do to regain what we lost. Being hurt by someone often threatens our safety. We don't want to feel weak or powerless to stop pain, so instead, we hold on to unforgiveness to regain power and keep ourselves safe.

The problem is that unforgiveness is an illusion of power because anger comes with it, and anger doesn't feel like weakness. Anger feels much safer than weakness, powerlessness, or pain. There's no vulnerability in anger, so we hold tight to unforgiveness, believing it to be the antidote to pain.

Jesus understands this temptation found in weakness. To be the perfect example for us, he had to experience all that we would. He had to be relatable and understand what it was to be tempted during his weakest moments, too. Jesus had to experience betrayal and yet not sin in response to it. By doing so, he demonstrates that we can do the same. The more we follow the example of Jesus instead of giving in to what we think provides safety, the more we realize our only true safety comes from him.

Like Jesus, you can be tempted when you feel weak and still choose to forgive. Unforgiveness isn't what keeps you safe. Jesus is.

For Relief and Peace

Taking Time to Notice (page 128) This exercise will help you take difficult emotions like anger, and first feel them, acknowledge them, and then give them to the Lord. You will find peace as you bring your biggest struggles into God's presence. Invite him to work in your life and sit in those struggles with you.

Dear Lord, Please help me not to be fooled by the illusion of unforgiveness. I want to follow your example. In Jesus' name. Amen.

Revenge Isn't as Good as It Seems

Dear friends, never take revenge. Leave that to the

righteous anger of God. For the Scriptures say,

"I will take revenge; I will pay them back,"

says the Lord.

ROMANS 12:19

Desiring payback comes up quite a bit in our counseling practice. It often presents itself as a path to feeling better, which is what most people who have been hurt want. It's understandable that revenge might relieve the pain we've experienced. There's something about retaliating that feels like the epitome of justice, and justice should make you feel better, right?

The problem is that revenge may make you think you will feel better afterward, but the reality is that revenge makes you feel miserable. You feel worse because going after that payback often takes you out of alignment with your morals. Instead of taking revenge when you've been hurt, give those feelings to the Lord, trusting him for the justice that only he can provide.

Shelly was a sweet girl whose boyfriend cheated on her with her best friend. She was so devastated that she shamed them both publicly on social media. She wanted everyone to know how awful they were, but this was also out of character for her. She once prided herself on the empathy and support she always showed others, but now, after posting, she felt bad about herself. While the post did make her boyfriend and best friend look bad, and it did get lots of attention, it also did nothing to stop her pain or make her feel better.

You, like Shelly, may also describe yourself as empathetic and supportive. Seeking revenge as she did would only make you feel worse about yourself. It will never accomplish what you hope it will.

For Relief and Peace

Write and Rip (page 136) In this exercise, grant yourself the freedom to share your deepest thoughts and pain. Take your anger, thoughts of revenge, and anything that doesn't feel right before the Lord and release them.

Dear Lord, I don't want to feel the need for revenge. I want to leave revenge for those who wronged me in your hands. In Jesus' name.

Amen.

The Regret of Unforgiveness

I have fought the good fight, I have finished the

race, and I have remained faithful.

2 TIMOTHY 4:7

On your deathbed, you will likely ponder the most important things in life. Many articles contain lists of the top ten regrets of those dying, and consistently, the regret of not forgiving is on them. When people have wronged you, you can forgive them and move forward, or choose not to and harbor resentment, continuing to walk in pain. It turns out that those who chose the path of living with resentment regretted it.

As Paul the Apostle is nearing the end of his life, he shares his perspective in 2 Timothy. What he found most important was that he fought the good fight, finished the race, and remained faithful. That's it. He didn't hold a grudge or refuse to forgive others for the pain they caused him.

While forgiving others is not easy, it is also not worth holding on to. You can learn from Paul and all the others who have gone before us that what matters most is being found faithful, even in forgiveness.

For Relief and Peace

Practicing Acceptance (page 171) Living with an unforgiving heart is a disservice to yourself. Accepting something that feels wrong is challenging and requires grace and patience with yourself. However hard it may be, this work is worth doing and a goal you can work toward. So much more peace is available to you in acceptance rather than in holding a grudge.

Dear Lord, Please help me to live out my days doing the things that honor you and bring you glory. In Jesus' name. Amen.

Giving Yourself Grace When Forgiveness Is Hard

God saved you by his grace when you believed. And
you can't take credit for this; it is a gift from God.
Salvation is not a reward for the good things we
have done, so none of us can boast about it.

EPHESIANS 2:8-9

Forgiving someone who has hurt you might be the last thing
you want to do. You might have swirling thoughts over the destruction
their actions have caused, the grief you feel, or the anger that bubbles
up inside you. When you don't think forgiveness is possible, there's
grace for that. There's grace for the in-betweens when you're stuck
between pain and forgiveness.

With the gift of salvation, God gave us grace and forgiveness
through Jesus. That same grace is available to us today. If the God of
all creation can be so gracious to you, perhaps offering yourself some
grace in this trial is okay, too. There is no reward for being the perfect
Christian who forgives easily. Nor is there condemnation when you
struggle to forgive. In Jesus, there is never condemnation (Romans
8:1). Give yourself permission to pause, to listen to the Lord, and to
invite him in to prepare your heart.

When you pressure yourself or try to force forgiveness too quickly, it will lack the sincerity it needs to be believable, even to you. You will end up with a heart that knows it wasn't authentic. You can be assured that God understands pain and what it does to a heart more than we ever could. He knows your struggle on this journey and will meet you with his grace. This doesn't mean you should sit and stew in unforgiveness or anger. Rather, go to the Lord and share your pain with him so you can have forgiveness in your heart. Give your fears to him and trust that he will meet you where you are.

For Relief and Peace

Exploring Forgiveness (page 154) Giving yourself grace on this forgiveness journey can be challenging. It's okay for things to move slowly—there is no need to rush the process. In this week's exercise, pause to evaluate your beliefs around forgiveness and find potential hang-ups that are making the process more difficult. You are not on this journey alone.

Dear Lord, I need your grace today. Help me not to be so hard on myself and allow myself the time I need as I do my best to be obedient to you. In Jesus' name. Amen.

The Most Frustrating Thing about Forgiveness

Then Peter came to him and asked, "Lord, how
often should I forgive someone who sins against
me? Seven times?" "No, not seven times," Jesus
replied, "but seventy times seven!"

MATTHEW 18:21-22

Hands down, the most challenging thing about forgiveness is
found in Matthew 18, where Jesus tells us that we must keep offering it
over and over again. Peter posed this question to Jesus, hoping to
appear virtuous for his willingness to forgive as much as seven times. In
Peter's day, he had been taught forgiveness was offered only three
times. Even seven times sounds more doable than four hundred and
ninety, doesn't it? Clearly this was not the news Peter wanted to hear,
nor the news we still want to hear today.

The significance of four hundred and ninety was that it represented
limitless forgiveness. Jesus said we are called to forgive others as much
as God forgives us. This does not mean we allow someone to cause us
harm flippantly while we keep forgiving them, but it does mean that we
shouldn't limit how much we forgive. Forgiving a husband or wife
hundreds of times throughout a marriage is often necessary—you

cannot forgive just three times. However, if someone has a pattern of hurting you, establishing appropriate boundaries are necessary. The recurring pain that we may be wrestling with does not negate our need to forgive. We must always separate our pain from the call to forgive.

Through the power of the Holy Spirit, this limitless amount of forgiveness is an opportunity to wake up each day and choose to focus on forgiveness once again. God is so merciful—he is not only willing to forgive us repeatedly, he is asking us to do the same thing.

For Relief and Peace

Practicing Acceptance (page 171) For believers, forgiving others is a way of life. The reality is that we will be miserable if we don't learn how to forgive. As you begin to practice acceptance in this week's exercise, you'll discover that letting go and forgiving freely allows you to move forward in peace.

Dear Lord, Thank you for always forgiving me.
Please give me a forgiving heart to forgive others
in the same way. In Jesus' name. Amen.

Toxic Forgiveness

Don't waste what is holy on people who are unholy.

Don't throw your pearls to pigs! They will trample

the pearls, then turn and attack you.

MATTHEW 7:6

Kyleigh and Kevin were high school sweethearts. The only problem was that after ten years of dating, they weren't even close to getting married as Kyleigh desired. For years, Kevin's rejection and lack of initiative toward their relationship hurt Kyleigh. The truth was that while things were good for them when they were younger, Kevin had changed. He became someone who frequently lied, lost his temper, and said harsh things to Kyleigh. Their relationship remained toxic like this for years.

Kyleigh minimized forgiveness by giving it automatically, without considering the significance of the wrongdoings. Out of her desperation and hope for Kevin to be the man she wanted him to be, she ended up in denial over the man he was. She allowed Kevin to influence her self-worth far more than God did. Yes, God commands us to forgive, but he doesn't call us to forgive so flippantly as Kyleigh did.

If you have found yourself forgiving repeatedly, you might be casting your pearls before the pigs. In Kyleigh's case, she gave Kevin her best; in return, he destroyed it by taking advantage of her forgiving heart. In Matthew 7, he tells us not to waste what is holy, and sometimes that's forgiveness on people who are unrepentant and unwilling to change. You don't have to keep setting yourself up to forgive continuously. The truth is that it's possible to forgive and keep your pearls, or in Kyleigh's case, to forgive and move on, trusting that her true worth was found in God and not in a man that treated her poorly.

For Relief and Peace

Wake Up Your Self-Worth (page 161) One of the best ways to avoid unhealthy relationships is to firmly know your identity in Christ. Focus on your God-given identity before anything else with this week's exercise. Starting your morning knowing who you are in Christ will provide the foundation you need to start your day and recognize anything that goes against the Word of God.

Dear Lord, Thank you for your desire to protect my heart by not asking me to give the best of myself to someone who doesn't appreciate it. In Jesus' name. Amen.

Conflict Avoidant Forgiveness

Obviously, I'm not trying to win the approval of people, but of God. If pleasing people were my goal, I would not be Christ's servant.

GALATIANS 1:10

Hi, I'm Chris, and I'm a people pleaser. Since I was a child, I made it my responsibility to ensure everyone around me was happy. I learned how to avoid conflict like the plague. The moment I noticed anyone was upset, it provoked my pleasing tendencies. Despite my feelings, I learned to put on a happy face early.

My tendency to please overflowed into my marriage. If Jamie was upset, I would quickly meet her needs. If we got into a fight, I was the one who always apologized. Whenever she did something wrong, I would immediately forgive her without hesitation. If she sensed something in me and asked if I was okay, my response was always, "Yes, I'm fine." I dismissed my own feelings and created a habit of forgiving and moving on. Forgiveness became something that I felt I owed everyone. I was using my quick forgiveness as a way to avoid conflict.

Conflict avoidance is not why God wants you or me to forgive. Scripture says that we can't strive to please others and God simultaneously. Give yourself the freedom to please God with your forgiveness. You don't need to offer it solely to prevent conflict or to please people.

For Relief and Peace

Reframing Conflict (page 169) You are not alone if conflict is something you would rather avoid. However, conflict is essential for healthy relationships so that you can speak freely and allow your thoughts and opinions to be heard. In this exercise, you will establish steps toward healthy conflict that you can apply in any relationship.

- -

Dear Lord, I want to please you more than I worry about pleasing others. Please help me to face my fears of conflict to honor you. In Jesus' name. Amen.

- -

Forgiving and Restoring in Marriage

But forget all that—it is nothing compared to what I

am going to do. For I am about to do something

new. See, I have already begun! Do you not see it? I

will make a pathway through the wilderness. I will

create rivers in the dry wasteland.

ISAIAH 43:18–19

Our dear friends, Brad and Lisa, experienced a very challenging season of life. Early on in their marriage, Lisa discovered that her husband was having an affair. She was heartbroken and devastated. They both believed their marriage was over and without God's intervention, it would have been. They were days away from divorcing when Brad had what he says was a pivotal moment in his life. The Lord made it clear that he needed to repent and plead with his wife for another chance. So he did.

While this was the most vulnerable thing Lisa had ever done, she was willing. Not because she trusted Brad but because she trusted the Lord. She knew through all the praying she had done that God would be able to bring redemption to them if he wanted to.

A lot of pain comes with betrayal; the only way to move forward is to know that the Lord is faithful. While Brad had to earn her trust back ultimately, Lisa needed to trust the Lord. She needed to believe he could make their marriage new or mend her heart if Brad broke it again.

Lisa and Brad were able to find the healing they longed for. Brad grew in his faith as he walked humbly and earned Lisa's trust. Lisa's heart for her husband softened as she learned to trust the Lord. The redemption they received is available for you, too. If you desire reconciliation and are willing to work at it, you can trust the Lord to make rivers in the wasteland, too. And even if you are the only one seeking redemption, God can create goodness in your life as well. He won't leave you in the wasteland.

For Relief and Peace

Motivation Chart (page 152) There can be a lot of fear when deciding whether to move forward after any type of betrayal. Going through this week's exercise will help you determine which step to take, and the potential risks or rewards that will come with your decision.

Dear Lord, Thank you for being a God who can make all things brand new. Help me to believe that restoration is possible. In Jesus' name. Amen.

Forgiving Does Not Equal Reconciliation

Prove by the way you live that you have repented of

your sins and turned to God.

MATTHEW 3:8

In the Christian community, we often think that forgiveness and reconciliation must go hand in hand. This is not the case. Nowhere in Scripture does God ask anyone to tolerate abuse or unhealthy behavior. Even when Jesus tells us to turn the other cheek, he is not asking us to be a doormat (Matthew 5:38-39). The reality is that we only have two cheeks. God isn't commanding us to be abused by the continuous turning of our cheeks over and over again.

Forgiveness is necessary for healing, but reconciliation is not. Forgiveness is up to you, but reconciling requires both parties. First, rebuilding trust starts with repentance and changed behavior. Unfortunately, some people aren't repentant or trustworthy, and in these circumstances, we should steer clear of them. You also want to keep in mind that even if a relationship can't be reconciled, you can still find peace within yourself. When you know that you have followed the Lord and done all that you can to offer forgiveness, you can live at peace.

If the wrong committed against you was abusive or criminal, there is no need to desire reconciliation. But this doesn't hinder you from forgiving, healing, and moving on in your own life. Forgiving releases you from the cycle of negative thoughts and mentally being tethered to something that has been harmful in your life. God does not ask you to be yoked to anyone who isn't repentant. You have been given the freedom to choose the people in your life with wisdom.

For Relief and Peace

Evaluating Healthy Boundaries (page 165) One of the best ways to determine if a relationship should be continued or restored is whether your boundaries are respected and honored within it. If a relationship is healthy, your opinions and thoughts will be welcomed, and your likes and dislikes will be valued. As you go through the process of evaluating healthy boundaries this week, clearly establish the current health of your relationship, and develop a plan to ensure its health if you move forward.

Dear Lord, Thank you for your protection over my well-being. Give me wisdom with whoever I allow in my life. In Jesus' name. Amen.

Acknowledging the Hurt

He will wipe away every tear from their eyes, and

there will be no more death or sorrow or crying or

pain. All these things are gone forever.

REVELATION 21:4

I, Jamie, grew up in a home where I longed for love. I wanted to feel safe, protected, and cared for, but as a child I never did. When I became a follower of Christ as an adult, one of the first things I did was learn to forgive my parents, primarily my mother. As freeing as that was, it didn't seem enough to completely heal. I still felt stuck.

What I discovered was that I was missing a piece of the forgiveness and healing puzzle: grief. I needed to know that it was okay to forgive my parents and acknowledge their limitations and at the same time recognize the trauma and loss that they caused me. I needed to grieve the loss of my childhood. I needed to set aside time to be angry about how much harder life was for me because of their actions. I could forgive them and still deal with the damage and pain.

When someone has harmed you, it's okay to feel all the pain of their wrongdoings. It's also all right to do what I did and get a therapist's help. There will soon be a day when tears are no more, and it's okay if today is not that day.

For Relief and Peace

Where Are You? (page 134) This exercise provides an opportunity to look inward and take an honest evaluation of your pain and its impact on you. Use this exercise to identify when and where you are experiencing stress, pain, or other negative emotions; experience those feelings with God and invite him to help you with them.

Dear Lord, I seek you today asking for your help in processing my pain and grief. Be near today, Lord. In Jesus' name. Amen.

Trusting God to Mend Your Heart

The Lord hears his people when they call to him for help. He rescues them from all their troubles. The Lord is close to the brokenhearted; he rescues those whose spirits are crushed. The righteous person faces many troubles, but the Lord comes to the rescue each time.

PSALM 34:17-19

I've gotten a front-row seat to many broken hearts. They repeatedly ask me through tearstained faces, "Will this ever get better?" My answer is always yes.

I remember one woman who was over a year into her divorce process. It was a divorce she never anticipated and never desired. Her husband had an alcohol problem and was making horrible life choices that affected not only her but also their children. Mere months after their separation, he seemed to be thriving. He had a new apartment and girlfriend and seemingly suffered no consequences for his decisions. Meanwhile, here she was on a therapist's couch, wondering if she would ever get through this horrible pain.

I reminded her of God's promise to heal the brokenhearted and rescue those whose spirits are crushed. No matter what her husband was doing or how he was processing things, she could cling to the hope of God's nearness and healing hand.

By seeking the Lord's help, she embraced the process of grief and forgiveness. She relied on God's timing for his perfect rescue to unfold and bring healing. In her own way, she is now thriving, not because her life is perfect, but because in her cries to the Lord for help, he answered. Day by day she was able to find God faithful, and it's a wonderful comfort to know that you can too.

For Relief and Peace

Practicing Worship (page 143) A foundational piece of trusting someone is knowing them and their character. When you are reminded of who God is, how much he cares for you, and how wonderful he always has been, it's easier to trust his work in your life. This week, trust God to mend your heart from a place of praise.

Dear Lord, You know the heaviness of my heart and that I need your healing. Give me the patience I need to wait for your rescue. In Jesus' name. Amen.

Trusting God's Justice

He is the Rock; his deeds are perfect. Everything he
does is just and fair. He is a faithful God who does
no wrong; how just and upright he is!

DEUTERONOMY 32:4

Jordan was a young mom who suffered the unthinkable.
She was wrongly accused of a crime she didn't commit. When she was
first accused, although traumatized, she felt secure in knowing that she
did not commit the heinous crime and that the truth would ultimately
reveal itself. Unfortunately, this wasn't the case. Error after error
happened during her trial. The prosecution gave misinformation to the
jurors and withheld facts. This trial to prove her innocence ended up
costing her entire life savings and landing her in prison with a guilty
verdict. By all accounts, she was the victim of a total lack of justice.

Eventually, Jordan was granted a retrial where the jurors could hear
the previously missing information, and she was finally set free after
nine long years behind bars. However, for Jordan, her justice came at a
high cost. She lost nine years of her life, memories with her daughter,
and her marriage. Even after finding true forgiveness in her heart for
all that she had been through, the reality is that justice on earth can
still seem unjust. And for many, justice never comes at all.

When earthly justice is limited or may not come, we can cling to the assurance that God is the ultimate judge. He sees every injustice we've ever suffered. He knows the hurt and pain others have caused, and one day, his full justice will prevail. So, while we have no guarantee of justice here on earth, we are comforted by our Father and know he is always watching out for us. For all those moments when life is unfair, he is always there for us to turn to.

For Relief and Peace

Visualizing God's Justice (page 148) Suffering an injustice can stop you in your tracks and keep you from moving forward. It is such a heavy weight to carry. In this week's exercise, be comforted knowing that God's justice will prevail when you don't get it here on earth. As you release the injustice to him, find freedom in remembering that his hands are far more capable of carrying the heavy burden of injustice than yours.

Dear Lord, Thank you for being a God who rights every wrong and brings justice where it is due. Help me to leave justice in your hands and move forward in peace. In Jesus' name. Amen.

The Power of Prayer to Heal

You can ask for anything in my name, and I will do

it, so that the Son can bring glory to the Father.

Yes, ask me for anything in my name, and I will do it.

JOHN 14:13-14

Prayer is one of the most underutilized gifts we have received. It's easy to cry out to God in desperation when we're in turmoil, but making prayer a daily habit is a different story. We're all tempted to turn to God as a genie in the bottle, but prayer is so much more than that.

Prayer is an opportunity to spend daily time with the Creator of the Universe, the Maker of Heaven and Earth. It's showing God that your relationship with him is important to you. Prayer is a time to seek his face and learn his voice. When we make time to be in fellowship with God, we are shifting our focus on him and what he desires for our lives, rather than on what we want or alleviating the pain that has happened to us.

John 14 isn't telling us that if we want something, we name it and claim it in prayer. God is saying that if we desire something that's in his will, it will be ours. While we can't rely on getting everything we want from God, when it does happen, we can trust that what we've received is in his will. Scripture is clear that forgiveness is indeed God's will. If you ask God to help you heal on this journey, he will.

For Relief and Peace

Victory Prayers (page 130) This exercise will help you claim the power of his living, active word that is as powerful as a double-edged sword. You will be reminded of the power to overcome painful circumstances that you have been given in Christ.

Dear Lord, Guide me so that I can follow and listen to your voice. In Jesus' name. Amen.

The God Who Sees You

Thereafter, Hagar used another name to refer to the Lord, who had spoken to her. She said, "You are the God who sees me." She also said, "Have I truly seen the One who sees me?"

GENESIS 16:13

While I, Jamie, was growing up in a dysfunctional home with alcoholism, abuse, and neglect, there were times when I got mad at God and wondered where he was and why he allowed so much pain in my life. Maybe you know this feeling, too. I knew he could have intervened, but instead, he allowed the harm to come, which was confusing because I knew he loved me.

I wish I knew the answer to why God allows terrible things to happen. I can only trust that one day, the things that make no sense here on earth will be apparent in eternity. The important thing is not looking for the answers to what we don't understand about God and instead to hold on to what we know about him.

In Genesis 16, we find Hagar, a scared, abused, pregnant slave woman on the run. I imagine she was wondering where God was, too. Then, an angel showed up and spoke to her. He didn't show up to give her answers. Instead, his presence reassured her that the Lord saw her. The hope you can cling to today is the same hope Hagar had. It is not found in having the answers but knowing that your suffering is seen by a God who loves you. When we know the ultimate justice lies with God, we can forgive, knowing that he sees everything that is happening with us.

For Relief and Peace

Taking Time to Notice (page 128) This exercise will remind you that you do not need to run from any pain because you have a God who is willing to remain in it with you. As you pause and slow down to observe all you may be feeling, you will find that God and the peace he offers will meet you right where you are.

Dear Lord, Thank you for being faithful and seeing me even when I don't understand your plan. In Jesus' name. Amen.

You're Not to Blame

So now there is no condemnation for those who

belong to Christ Jesus.

ROMANS 8:1

Some wounds we carry are from traumatic events and have lifelong consequences. In those situations where trauma is involved, it can become hard to live a non-disrupted or "normal" life and blaming yourself for what has happened makes it worse.

Some people struggle to heal from the heinous things, even criminal, that have happened to them. In those situations, forgiveness is not the starting place. Instead, getting the needed and deserved help is the place to begin. Some traumas that individuals have experienced need professional help to overcome, and there is no shame in that. There is also no shame in identifying as a victim.

Jesus tells us there is no shame or condemnation for those who believe in him. He bore our shame on the cross so we wouldn't have to endure it. That includes the shame you might feel from being a victim. Jesus knew we would be prone to blaming ourselves for things beyond our control. The situation doesn't matter; no one ever asks to be victimized. The blame always falls on the abuser, not the victim. You don't have to fall into the trap of shame. Jesus already set you free.

For Relief and Peace

Letter to Self (page 141) In this week's exercise, you can gain a new perspective as you write a letter to yourself. As you explore what you might say to your younger self or future self, see yourself in a new light as a child who didn't know better and did the best they could; or as your future self who is thriving because of what God will teach you through the pain you experienced.

Dear Lord, It can be easy to blame myself for things that are not mine. Please help me to remain in you—where there is no condemnation. In Jesus' name. Amen.

Pain Is Temporary

For our present troubles are small and won't last

very long. Yet they produce for us a glory that

vastly outweighs them and will last forever.

2 CORINTHIANS 4:17

Stacy's forgiveness journey with her mother was a long one. After being hurt and disappointed repeatedly through the years, she struggled to feel anything other than betrayal and frustration. The pain her mother caused was more than Stacy could bear. Unfortunately, the lack of a willingness to change and the disregard for Stacy's boundaries led her to sever their relationship. As soon as their relationship ended, Stacy felt deep sorrow. Her mother had broken her heart.

Any kind of loss, even letting go of a toxic relationship, leads to a broken heart. However, as hard as this truth is to grasp in those moments of pain, Scripture tells us that our present pains and troubles are small and temporary. This isn't Jesus dismissing or making light of our suffering. He is reminding us that even though our problems don't seem small and temporary, in comparison to the eternal glory that is coming, they are.

This world we live in will not continue forever, nor will our pain. A day is coming when we will see how insignificant our most painful times were. Until this glory is revealed, we can rest in the knowledge that we can take Jesus at his word.

For Relief and Peace

Gaining Hope and Confidence during Dark Times (page 137) Suffering can feel like it lasts forever; it can also feel like too much to bear. When this is the case, it's best to take your weary and fearful heart and hide in the shelter of the Most High God. In this week's exercise, take your deepest fears and pain to the Lord. Remember who he is, the power he holds, and the comfort and safety he offers you. Dig deep in his Word, sit at his feet, and be comforted and refueled by his love.

Dear Lord, Help me see this season of pain from your perspective while I wait for your glory to be revealed. In Jesus' name. Amen.

Suffering Is a Process

In his kindness God called you to share in his
eternal glory by means of Christ Jesus. So
after you have suffered a little while, he will
restore, support, and strengthen you, and
he will place you on a firm foundation.

1 PETER 5:10

Whether you have a knee-jerk reaction to run from or even numb suffering, it has a greater refining purpose and can teach us to trust God and others in a loving community. It can even bring healing. When we are in community with one another, it's painful to watch others suffer, which can also be true for the one who caused it.

As counselors who work with married couples, whenever an affair has taken place and healing work has started, it's common for the betraying spouse to rush the betrayed spouse forward. They grow weary of watching their spouse struggle with pain, forgiveness, and repeated triggers, often pushing them to get over it. They also often want to assuage their own guilt and move on. It's essential for you to know that whether you're recovering from infidelity or another kind of betrayal, you don't have to allow yourself to be pushed forward sooner than you're ready.

A new foundation of healing can't be built upon the rubble of suffering that's been ignored. You can't heal from pain you've never given yourself permission to feel. Although unpleasant, we can endure temporary suffering because strength and restoration is waiting for us. God walks with us through our pain and guides us down the road of true healing and forgiveness.

For Relief and Peace

Where Are You? (page 134) In this week's exercise, learn how to process your suffering rather than running from or numbing it out. When you take the time to pause, look inward and bring that pain to the Lord.

Dear Lord, Please help me through my suffering and to move forward. Use my time of suffering to rebuild a firm foundation. In Jesus' name. Amen.

It's Okay Not to Be Okay

Each time he said, "My grace is all you need, My
power works best in weakness." So now I am glad to
boast about my weakness, so that the power of
Christ can work through me.

2 CORINTHIANS 12:9

Do you say, "I'm fine" or "It's okay," as flippantly as we both do?
It's uncomfortable to admit that you're hurting or not doing okay. It's
important for you to know that you're allowed to feel however you
need to, especially if you need time to figure out your feelings.

Nothing is unbiblical about feeling sad, hurt, or having difficulty
getting over something. The Psalms are full of lamentations and
people crying out to God in pain.

God graciously reassures us that we are free to be weak, and even
invites us to be in weakness. And although feeling sad or hurt often
feels like weakness, know that it is courageous. In those moments, we
can boldly admit to God that we are not perfect; it's okay to cry, be
mad, or take some time for yourself. This is where Christ meets you
with his power and offers his strength to overcome those challenges.

When you choose to forgive that doesn't make the pain instantly
disappear; that expectation often only worsens it. If you're struggling

with feeling weak when you're still hurting, keep this in mind: It's okay not to be okay. God's strength will get you through.

For Relief and Peace

Identifying an Ideal Friend (page 159) If you're in a season where you don't feel okay, letting others in is important. God will always be there for you, providing a listening and compassionate ear, but he also longs for you to live in fellowship and relationship with others. In this week's exercise, as you identify what a true friend might look like based on Scripture, you will learn it's good to let others in to help.

Dear Lord, Thank you for giving me the freedom to be hurt and for giving me your strength to endure it. In Jesus' name. Amen.

Stuck in the In-Between

Jesus Christ is the same yesterday,

today, and forever.

HEBREWS 13:8

There's a piece of the forgiveness journey that doesn't always get spoken about: the in-between space. You're unsure whether to move on or turn back in this space. Both choices seem equally horrifying. Part of you wants to forgive and run back, but the other part wants to move on and forget about this painful part of your life forever. And no matter how much you contemplate all the scenarios, you can't find the correct answer.

This in-between space can be a search for a guarantee. The belief is that if you make the right choice, you can avoid pain and won't be hurt again. The problem is that there is no such guarantee available. And no matter how much time you give it, the answer may never reveal itself. But we can have faith in one guarantee you can always trust—knowing that Jesus will be the same today as he will be tomorrow.

If you're stuck in this in-between space, know that it's supposed to feel uneasy and confusing. Your heart has been hurt, and the guarantee you're searching for is a normal response to that hurt. In times like this, be encouraged that although people may fail you again, Jesus never will.

For Relief and Peace

Attributes of God (page 163) When you find yourself stuck or in a place of insecurity, remember that no matter where you are or what decision you make, God is with you. He is faithful, he is steadfast, and he is powerful enough to carry you through life's hardest trials. As you complete this week's exercise, your heart will be filled with reminders of how powerful and faithful God is in all circumstances.

Dear Lord, Thank you for always being trustworthy. Please help me to rely on you to protect my fearful heart. In Jesus' name. Amen.

Sharing Your Burdens

Share each other's burdens,

and in this way obey the law of Christ.

GALATIANS 8:2

Chris and I both avoid seeking help for different reasons. When I have been hurt, I desire to fix it myself or suffer alone. Chris, on the other hand, fears burdening anyone with his pain and pushes it beneath the surface. Neither of our flawed approaches was abiding by Christ's design and law.

God made others to be an encouragement to you. He created people to come alongside you to share and help carry your burdens. You aren't meant to suffer alone. If you have wounds that you've been trying to handle alone or push beneath the surface, that isn't what God wants for you. He wants you to be supported. Your best healing will come from allowing others to share in your pain.

When someone has caused you harm, you will get through it better with the help of a trusted friend, spouse, or family member. Your pain is not a burden you should have to carry alone; according to Scripture, it's even an opportunity for your loved one to fulfill the law of Christ. Sharing your pain is good for you and for them.

For Relief and Peace

Identifying an Ideal Friend (page 159) As you work through this week's exercise, see what Scripture says about good traits found in friends. You will also identify what an ideal friend might look like to you. During difficult times, when you invite others in to help carry your burdens and share your heart, your endurance will expand as you share the weight with a compassionate friend.

Dear Lord, Please help me find someone with whom I can safely share my pain with. I don't want to go through healing alone. In Jesus' name. Amen.

The Impact of Trauma

He will cover you with his feathers. He will

shelter you with his wings. His faithful promises

are your armor and protection. Do not be

afraid of the terrors of the night, nor the

arrow that flies in the day.

PSALM 91:4-5

Trauma can be acute, chronic, or complex. You can be acutely traumatized by a one-time event, such as a bad wounding from a friend, or chronically traumatized by the same repeated events, like ongoing relational abuse that takes place in abusive or dysfunctional homes.

It's important that trauma is dealt with in a healthy way and prioritized, as it affects your emotional well-being and makes forgiveness difficult. When you've experienced trauma, you can feel the effects of it physically. It can remain trapped in your body and wreak havoc, cause you to shut down emotionally and withdraw, and lead you to destructive behavior and dysfunctional relationships. Trauma can also cause hyper-vigilance and a dysregulated nervous system, which can result in depression, anxiety, difficulty concentrating, changes in sleep patterns, and other afflicted symptoms. These troubles are all common trauma responses.

The good news is that there is real hope if you've experienced trauma. God will always provide a safe hiding place for you while you work all of it out, either with him, a therapist, or a physician. His shelter will completely cover you day or night and provide the protection and safety you long for. Pause forgiveness if you need to, hide under the wings of the Lord, and get the support you need.

For Relief and Peace

Finding Peace in Nature (page 124) This week's exercise will foster healthy mental and emotional well-being. Safely process any trauma during your alone time with God. There is no need to push yourself. You will have complete control over how little or how much you want to explore your pain and process it with the Lord.

Dear Lord, Thank you for hiding me in your wings. Please reveal to me if I need help healing from trauma. In Jesus' name. Amen.

Don't Defend Those Who Hurt You

When I was a child, I spoke and thought and reasoned as a child. But when I grew up, I put away childish things.

1 CORINTHIANS 13:11

Do you know anyone who seems to see the good in everyone? If someone cuts them off in traffic, they respond by considering how bad of a day that person might be having. If their friend is late, they justify it by assuming they had something important come up. While the tendency to see the good is not necessarily a bad trait in these situations, it is a trait that is worth evaluating. It's one thing to dismiss being cut off in traffic. But maybe the friend who is always late might not deserve you making another excuse for them.

When someone needs forgiveness, you must let them own up to their actions. You may be that person who tends to trust in the good of everyone, but having this trait doesn't always help the other person mature or become responsible. God expects us to take personal responsibility. The Lord tells adults to act like adults and put off their childish ways; a child doesn't take responsibility for the wrongs they have done.

Even if the one who has hurt you has a justifiable excuse for why they caused you harm, that does not negate them from owning it. Instead of defending them, let them take ownership of their actions. The Bible talks about allowing people to experience the consequences of their actions (Galatians 6:7).

For Relief and Peace

Reframing Conflict (page 169) Conflict can occur when a guilty party refuses to take responsibility for their actions. If this is the case, it is not helpful to simply sweep it under the rug. If you view conflict improperly or fear it, you may find it easier to justify the wrongdoing instead of addressing an issue that seems impossible to resolve. In this week's exercise, understand how you view conflict and learn appropriate and healthy ways to engage in it, even when solutions can't be found.

Dear Lord, Please help me see that I don't need to defend those who hurt me. Help me separate myself and allow them to take responsibility for themselves. In Jesus' name. Amen.

Wounds from a Loved One

Now Jesus was deeply troubled, and he exclaimed,

"I tell you the truth, one of you will betray me!"

JOHN 13:21

We don't often see Jesus distressed in Scripture. But when he is about to be betrayed by his friend Judas, a man he dearly loved, we see how deeply troubled he is. Moments before Jesus said these words in the book of John, he was washing his disciples' feet, including those of Judas. Jesus was humbling himself while Judas was preparing to exalt himself.

Think about this for a moment. Jesus was about to go through the most agonizing pain he's ever been through. He was about to be seized for the crucifixion, not because society sold him out but because his friend did. Even knowing that this was part of the ultimate plan, Jesus was still troubled and hurt.

When we are hurt by a loved one, the pain is intensified because we expect more from those who claim to love us. After all, they are the ones who should be protecting us, not harming us. When loved ones disappoint or betray us, we fall much farther than if a stranger or acquaintance were to let us down. If your heart feels extra wounded because of a betrayal by a loved one, find comfort in knowing that Jesus also understands that same kind of betrayal.

For Relief and Peace

Where Are You? (page 134) When you have been wounded by a person whom you would normally go to for love and support, it's hard to know where to turn. As you work through this week's exercise, take practical steps to bring your deep pains to the Lord and allow him to be the comforter and healer of your heart.

Dear Lord, Thank you for being a God who understands what it is to be hurt by a friend. Please heal me from this painful wound. In Jesus' name. Amen.

Being Grateful After Being Hurt

Be thankful in all circumstances, for this is God's will

for you who belong to Christ Jesus.

1 THESSALONIANS 5:18

Sometimes Scripture can be frustrating and confusing, and verses like 1 Thessalonians 5:18 might be one. What do you mean, God? You want me to be thankful even though I've been hurt? Well, as confusing as it is, the answer is yes. But there's a reason he calls us to be grateful even in our suffering. It's because gratefulness is good for us, good for the Kingdom, and it's a gift we can choose, even when we're hurting.

You may not have been given a choice about what happened to you, but you can choose how you will respond to it, and your choice matters. Gratefulness does not need to be your first response, nor should it be, but eventually, it does need to become a response. When you choose to be grateful for everything that comes into your life, you're choosing to trust in the sovereignty of God. You're also choosing to shift your focus from your pain onto the goodness of God. We can also choose to focus on the good things that are happening in our lives, despite our wounding.

Developing a grateful heart means not letting suffering inflict more pain than necessary, showing the Lord your ultimate trust in him with your life, even in your deepest pain.

For Relief and Peace

Gratitude List (page 132) It can be difficult to see what is good in your life when it feels like everything is going wrong. This week's exercise will help you to remember that despite the magnitude of your pain, God is still good, and your life is still rich with blessings, both big and small.

Dear Lord, Please heal my heart and fill it with gratefulness, even when I have been wronged.

In Jesus' name. Amen.

WEEK 46

Winning the Battle Over Your Negative Thoughts

We are human, but we don't wage war as humans do. We use God's mighty weapons, not worldly weapons, to knock down the strongholds of human reasoning and to destroy false arguments. We destroy every proud obstacle that keeps people from knowing God. We capture their rebellious thoughts and teach them to obey Christ.

2 CORINTHIANS 10:3–5

Have you ever observed your tendencies in your thought processes? Your thoughts are very powerful, and often, your mind is a battlefield. In 2 Corinthians 10, Paul uses such strong military language because he understands the magnitude of this battle in the spiritual realm. A battle that your mental realm can become a part of.

The enemy loves to feed us lies, to tempt us not to forgive, to hold on to anger, or whatever else he can use to keep us from walking in truth and to keep others from seeing God in our lives. If you constantly think about the wrongs done to you, how hopeless you feel, the

revenge you'd like to see come to fruition, or anything else that's harmful, you are fighting on the wrong side of the battle.

What God says to do instead of ruminating on the negative is to
take those thoughts captive, much like a prisoner of war is taken
captive, and make them obedient to Christ. Those negative thoughts
are leading you astray. They are not reminding you of Christ's truth
that redemption and hope are possible, that forgiving is freeing, and
God's way is best. Those negative thoughts you have don't have to
destroy you. You can destroy *them*.

For Relief and Peace

How to Stop Ruminating (page 167) Everyone is susceptible to letting
negative thoughts take over their minds, especially when trauma
occurs or when we enter a challenging season of life. This week's
exercise will help you identify when negative thoughts are becoming a
pattern and how to acknowledge your real fears and worries. When
you do this, you will keep negativity from taking over while replacing
any lies you believe with truth.

Dear Lord, Please help me to take captive every

negative thought I have and release it to you.

In Jesus' name. Amen.

Worshipping While You Wait

No one is holy like the Lord! There is no one besides you; there is no Rock like our God.

1 SAMUEL 2:2

There are two things we tell almost every client we see at some point during their time in counseling: to journal and to turn on worship music. Inevitably, when we hear back from them, both things have brought value to their lives. Journaling helps you process. It slows and quiets your brain, allowing you to work things out more clearly. Worship lifts your spirit and changes your brain chemistry by increasing levels of serotonin, dopamine, and endorphins—similar to what antidepressants do. It also has a lot of spiritual value.

Being on a journey of forgiveness is often draining. It's hard and heavy work. Taking the time to worship can alleviate much of the heaviness. When you pause to worship, you focus on God instead of your problems. Worship helps you remember who God is. When you sing about his holiness and all his attributes, like being the Rock of Ages, you become aware of how big he is and how capable he is of carrying you through this difficult time. There is no one like him and reflecting on it can be relief for a weary heart.

Worship fills your heart with gratefulness and refreshes your soul. If you want your struggles to feel smaller, stack them against a great big God.

For Relief and Peace

Practicing Worship (page 143) It can be hard to be patient while waiting for hard times to pass or for healing to come. This week's exercise will ease your waiting by focusing on worship and reminding your heart that God is sovereign and in control.

Dear Lord, Today, I want to praise you for being faithful, sovereign, and holy. Help me remember who you are while I'm struggling. In Jesus' name. Amen.

Sustaining a Forgiving Heart

"Get out of here Satan," Jesus told him. "For the Scriptures say, 'You must worship the Lord your God and serve only him.'"

MATTHEW 4:10

Forgiveness can be a battle, and the reality of most battles is that they aren't usually won with one-time knockouts. You will likely have a few rounds with the enemy while trying to maintain a forgiving heart. Even Jesus himself, when he was tested by Satan in the wilderness, went a few rounds. Three times the enemy kept at him, tempting Jesus to align with him; but every time, Jesus refused and reminded Satan of God's Word.

One of the best ways to remain forgiving when you're tempted to give in to anger, bitterness, or revenge is to forbid the enemy a say in your life. He will remind you of the wrongs against you and tempt you to seek justice. He will tell you God's path is too hard and that his way is better. He is the father of lies and will say whatever he needs to say to change your heart. But his way is a lie, and you must remember that your best knockout punch is God's Word. The more you are grounded in God's Word, the more you can recognize the enemy's lies and refute them.

When you know Scripture and have it memorized, it will become your greatest weapon. An easy first step is to write a meaningful verse out and put it where you can see it throughout your day on a sticky note, a three-by-five card, or your phone wallpaper. Recite it to yourself every time you notice it. Like Jesus in the wilderness, you can throw the truth of God's living and active Word in the enemy's face and tell him to take a hike.

For Relief and Peace

Steps to Sustaining Forgiveness (page 126) This week's exercise offers practical ways to keep forgiveness at the forefront of your mind using the acronym FORGIVE. Focus on each practical building block step-by-step and move through the process of forgiving someone.

Dear Lord, May I hide your Word in my heart and always be prepared to stand my ground in this battle. In Jesus' name. Amen.

Be Transformed by God

Don't copy the behaviors and customs of
this world, but let God transform you into a
new person by changing the way you think.
Then you will learn to know God's will for you,
which is good and pleasing and perfect.

ROMANS 12:2

When we've been hurt, or our trust has been broken, it's easy to believe that good things or good people don't exist. If we're not careful, we can allow the world and its sinful ways to make us jaded, changing who we are and how we think.

Instead of letting the world's ways change us, we should allow God to do it. If we allow pain to transform us into someone who no longer trusts people, has walls up, or refuses to let others close to us, we will never be able to discern the good, pleasing, and perfect will of God. He can take our pain and use it to teach us and make us grow.

God wants good things for us. He wants us to know his will and to live in it. He wants us to look to *him* to be transformed, not to a faulty world. Pain will always try to change you—especially how you think—but God reminds us that that is his job.

For Relief and Peace

God's Truth (page 139) It's worth it to take the time to get to know who God is instead of focusing only on what he can do for you, because it can transform your life. As you go through this week's exercise, you will find that the more you get to know God, the easier it will be to hear his voice, follow his will, and trust what he says to be true.

Dear Lord, You are the only one that can ultimately transform my life. Help me change only by and through you, and not the world. In Jesus' name. Amen.

God's Plan for You Wins

You intended to harm me, but God intended it all
for good. He brought me to this position so I could
save the lives of many people.

GENESIS 50:20

In chapters 37–50 of Genesis, the story of Joseph unfolds.
Joseph was the youngest brother, their father's favorite, and was
disliked by his eleven older brothers. To add to their jealousy, he shared
a prophetic dream he had where he ruled over them, and they bowed
down to him. Joseph's dream seemed more like a nightmare to his
brothers, so they schemed and plotted to get rid of him.

Joseph was betrayed by his brothers and sold into slavery. This one
act led to many devastating events for Joseph, including false accusa-
tions and time in prison. After his whole life was turned upside down,
Joseph knew what it was like to be deeply hurt and still called to
forgive.

When the time came years later for Joseph to reunite with his
brothers, he didn't meet them with vengeance or anger. Joseph had
already followed God's leading through forgiveness and knew his
brothers' cruelty didn't get the final say. Just like in Joseph's story, God
is the only one who gets the last word in your story, too. He can take
what someone has done to harm you and use it for good. In Joseph's

case, he ultimately ended up in a position of power where he saved his family and others from a great famine. Your suffering won't be for naught. God will eventually make something good out of it.

For Relief and Peace

Making Time to Celebrate (page 150) How reassuring it is to know that God's intentions for you are good. He can take what the enemy intends for harm and flip it on its head. In this week's exercise, explore some of the goodness that can come after you feel attacked by the enemy.

Dear Lord, Please help me to trust that your plan for me is coming to fruition and that it is the only one that matters. In Jesus' name. Amen.

Finding Joy Again

You haven't done this before. Ask, using my name,

and you will receive, and you will have abundant joy.

JOHN 16:24

On many occasions, Jesus instructed his followers to pray and even taught them how to pray. Still, John 16:24 marks the first time he's ever told them to pray using the authority of his name. Though it may seem like he's offering himself as a magic genie so that we can receive whatever we request, that isn't so. When we pray in Jesus's name, we do so harmoniously with his will. Not everything we ask for will be within God's will, but we know that having joy is!

God doesn't want us wallowing in misery forever. He wants our joy to return. It will show the world what it's like to follow a God who gives us joy abundantly. It's one of the many gifts he gives his children.

To find your joy again, you must set down your fears and become vulnerable. Embracing the risk of being hurt again means opening yourself to the possibility of true healing and restoration. By living with vulnerability, you invite God into every aspect of your journey, trusting in his love and provision. With the authority of Jesus' name, you can approach God confidently, knowing that he hears your prayers and cares for your needs. Surrendering your concerns releases the burden of worry to him, allowing you to experience the freedom and peace that comes from trusting in his plan for your life.

For Relief and Peace

Filling Your Joy Bucket (page 145) Going through stressful situations or hard seasons can drain your joy, leaving you feeling depleted, sad, or even depressed. In this week's exercise, learn to experience joy again and with intention. When you can find daily joy, handling the stressors of life is manageable.

Dear Lord, I need joy, Lord, fill me with it abundantly. In Jesus' name. Amen.

Victory of the Forgiver

No, despite all these things, overwhelming victory

is ours through Christ, who loved us.

ROMANS 8:37

Our children used to play sports, and on occasion, one team's score would be so far ahead that there was no chance of catching up. Depending on whose team you were on, the scoreboard could be pretty embarrassing. Those games almost felt pointless, and by the end, there wasn't just a winning team. There was an overwhelmingly victorious team.

When you choose to forgive, you are overwhelmingly victorious as well. Your opponent, the enemy, or anyone he has used to hurt you has nothing on you. In Christ, you are more than a conqueror. Nothing can snatch you out of God's hand, and nothing here on earth can destroy you. You stand firm in that victory when you choose forgiveness. You are declaring that no act of evil against you gets to score.

Forgiving someone who has hurt you is a declaration that you are untouchable as a follower of Christ. It is knowing that you can face life's trials and being confident that you will come out winning. After all, the team you play for is stacked with the Creator of the Universe.

For Relief and Peace

Making Time to Celebrate (page 150) The forgiveness journey can feel long and daunting. And while God tells us we are victorious in him, you may not feel the victory until you are on the other side of the journey. With this exercise, see the light at the end of the tunnel and celebrate victory.

Dear Lord, When I feel like I am losing, remind me that I am more than a conqueror—you made me victorious. In Jesus' name. Amen.

PART II

FAITH-GUIDED SKILLS FOR LIVING OUT PEACE

Removing Barriers to Forgiveness

Removing any obstacles that may be preventing you
from being able to forgive.

TIME

20 minutes to answer and reflect

INSTRUCTIONS

People struggle to forgive or are unable to forgive for various reasons. Those reasons will remain a mystery if we don't examine them. Often, the decisions we make are based on our pain, what we understand about God, or what we were taught in our family of origin.

In this exercise, rely on the Lord to help uncover hidden roadblocks that keep or make it difficult for you from forgiving. Before you begin, first take a moment to pray and ask the Lord to reveal any unhealthy beliefs or barriers that are keeping you from his will in your life.

1. To begin, choose one to three barriers from the list below that you currently struggle with, or add one of your own.

    - I don't know how to forgive.
    - I don't like thinking about the incident and would rather deny that it happened.
    - I feel guilty that this event happened.
    - There will be no justice if I forgive.
    - I shouldn't have to forgive if there has been no apology.
    - I am mad and refuse to forgive.
    - My offender doesn't deserve my forgiveness.
    - If I forgive, I will only be hurt again.

- I don't understand forgiveness.
- If I forgive them, it means what happened was okay.

2. Reflect on your selected barriers and why those particular barriers are hard for you. This could be because of a past experience, something you were taught or saw modeled, or it might be unique to the situation you are currently facing.
3. On a separate piece of paper, write down what God is revealing to you and ask for his help in overcoming this barrier. Simply talk to him as you would a friend, ask for his help, and write down what he is telling you.
4. Anytime you face this barrier, remember to ask for the Lord's help in knocking it down.

··· *TIP* ·······································

If you get stuck, don't forget to invite the Lord to bring whatever you need to learn to the surface. Pause long enough to listen to him.

Finding Peace in Nature

Calming your body and experiencing the many
benefits of nature and bodily movement.

30 minutes daily or as desired

Psalm 19:1 tells us, "The heavens proclaim the glory of God. The skies display his craftsmanship." Getting out in nature, even just for a bit to reflect, provides a great reminder of who God is and all he can do. It is so good to remember how big he is, especially when you are in pain and need his healing. Sometimes, the sun on your face is enough to change your mood and lift your spirits while processing heavy things.

When you combine nature with just a 30-minute walk, you can reap even more benefits. You will have increased energy, an improved sense of well-being, less sadness, anxiety, depression, and lower stress levels. Whether you sit outside and gaze at creation or get your blood pumping through a walk, the benefits you receive will help clear your head and process any pain.

1. Find a nice spot to sit outside. Go to a local park, the beach, or a pretty place on your deck, patio, or in your yard if that is available.
2. Dedicate 30 minutes to sit and clear your head while you soak in the sun, the skies, and all that is around you.

3. If it doesn't feel like too much, share with the Lord all the pain you've been experiencing. This can be a time to let out all the heavy emotions you've been feeling or a simple time to bask in his presence. You are in control of what you want to share with the Lord. He can handle it.

OPTION TO MOVE

1. Go on a walk at a local park or in your neighborhood.
2. Dedicate 30 minutes to move your body at whatever pace is comfortable. Use this time to talk to the Lord about the trauma you've experienced. Seek his heart for comfort, healing, and guidance for any next steps you may need to take to further support your journey.
3. Remember, you are in control and do not need to push yourself further than you feel comfortable going.

TIP

If the weather doesn't permit or if you cannot go for a walk, or allot 30 minutes, find a window to stand in front of and embrace the outdoors. You may also move your body indoors to get the benefits of physical activity.

Steps to Sustaining Forgiveness

Giving you specific focus areas for developing a biblical mindset to maintain a heart of forgiveness.

5 to 10 minutes

Most difficult things aren't usually conquered and mastered on the first try. With all the challenges that come with forgiveness, it's helpful to refresh your mind or repeatedly return and start again. As you learn what each letter represents in the acronym FORGIVE, focus on one specific letter that stands out to you or take the time to learn all of them. You may need to keep returning to one letter, which is fine. Forgiveness is a process, and so is sustaining it.

Choose a letter and definition and write it down so you can pull it out and read it throughout the day.

F—Forbid. Forbid any negative recurring thoughts to keep circling in your mind. As soon as they enter, say to yourself—aloud if possible—"I refuse to let these thoughts take up space in my mind."

O—Overcome. Overcome the temptation to keep rehashing the event, a conversation with the offender, or any confrontations that have taken place. Instead, focus on holding your tongue and allowing space for the Holy Spirit to bring conviction of any wrongdoing.

R—Repeat Scripture. Choose a Bible verse that speaks to you or your situation and claim it. Work to memorize it, write it in a notes app on your phone or on a piece of paper you can carry. Take advantage of God's living and active Word and allow it to work in your life.

G—Give. Give the situation and your pain over to God as often as necessary. You will be tempted to keep taking it back; if you do, cast it on the Lord once again. Repeat this as often as you need to.

I—Intercede. Intercede for your offender. Pray for them. Ask God to give you his heart for them.

V—Value. Value giving over receiving. Take your focus off yourself and what you need and find someone else to give it to. This can be words of affirmation, intercessory prayer, or a tangible gift. If appropriate, you can do this for the one you are trying to forgive.

E—Extend. Extend God's grace and mercy. Ask God to help you express to others the same grace and mercy he extends to you.

························· *TIP* ·························

If any step is too difficult, don't just immediately skip over it. Ask the Lord for help so that you can receive it and learn from it before you move on.

Taking Time to Notice

.... USEFUL FOR ....

Training yourself to be present in your body and inviting
the peace of God into your pain.

.... TIME ....

5 to 10 minutes

.... INSTRUCTIONS ....

"Notice that" is one of the most common phrases used by trauma
therapists, and with good reason. Most people who have been hurt in
some way tend to want to breeze by the hard parts. We don't want to
experience fearful thoughts. We don't want the stomachaches, head-
aches, or tension in our shoulders. The reality is that God created your
mind, soul, and body. When we learn to listen to every part that
speaks, we learn to trust the Lord to bring healing.

This grounding exercise will help you invite in the peace and calm
of the Lord.

1. Identify one consistent thought that keeps coming back to your
    mind regarding your situation. Examples: "I feel so embar-
    rassed," "I will never get over this," or "I can't believe they hurt
    me like this."
2. Sit up straight with your feet planted firmly on the ground.
    Breathe in, fill your belly with air, and let it all out. Do this
    3–4 times.
3. Recall the thought you chose from step one. While you think
    about that, notice how your body feels when you dwell on that
    thought. What sensations do you have? Scan your body from

head to toe and tune in to anything you feel. Maybe it's a knot in your neck, a clenched jaw, a heaviness in your chest.

4. When you notice your bodily sensations, what feelings are coming to mind? Are you feeling hopeless or anxious? Abandonment or betrayal?

5. Once you've named your feelings, pause to acknowledge them. You don't have to react to them or run away from them. Allow yourself to feel them.

6. Name those feelings again and use this prayer, "Lord, I am feeling 'anxious.' Will you sit with me in this feeling until it passes? Help me to feel safe with you while you heal my mind. In Jesus' name. Amen." Repeat this prayer with every emotion you feel.

.... *TIP* ....

As you work through this process of becoming more attuned to your feelings and body, focus on your breathing throughout the entire exercise, using the breathing technique in step 2. Repeat this exercise as often as you need to throughout the week ahead.

Victory Prayers

Helping you confront and release anything that's keeping you from experiencing the freedom of forgiveness.

5 to 10 minutes

When you pray God's Word, you are putting a sword in the hands of the Holy Spirit. You are engaging in a spiritual battle where you are on the winning side. As you engage in these prayers, you can trust that God will be at work in your life. Your prayers, especially the ones rooted in Scripture, are like guided arrows going after any target the enemy has put in your life. You can trust that your prayers are untouchable by the enemy. He can't stop you from praying, nor can he defend himself against your prayers. When you claim the truth of Scripture, the victory will be yours.

To get started, find a comfortable place to pray where you can have some quiet and uninterrupted time.

VICTORY-CONQUERING PRAYERS

I lay my life at your feet and surrender to your will and plan for me. (Jeremiah 29:11)

I reject any thoughts that are not from you or that don't align with your word. (2 Corinthians 10:3-5)

I am standing in the full armor of God and asking you to bind the Enemy and his demonic forces from having any influence on me. (Ephesians 6:11)

I reject any ungodly and unforgiving thought trying to defeat me. (Ephesians 6:16)

I choose to forgive anyone who has caused me pain, and I release to you all of the anger and pain that I am feeling. (Colossians 3:13)

I resist the devil and all that he is trying to do in my life and declare that he must flee. (James 4:7)

Thank you, Jesus, that you who lives in me is greater than the enemy of this world. Help me to live undefeated against a spirit of unforgiveness. (1 John 4:4)

In Jesus' name. Amen.

.... *TIP* ....

If you want to spend more time in prayer or take your prayers deeper, grab your Bible and a notebook and write each Scripture and prayer, expanding on it as you feel led.

Gratitude List

Developing a healthy mindset shaped by
gratitude rather than loss or pain.

5 to 15 minutes

The Lord tells us in 1 Thessalonians 5:16–18 that we should give thanks in all circumstances. He also tells us in Colossians 3:15 that thankfulness is a part of allowing the peace of Christ to rule in our hearts. In this exercise, pursue peace by intentionally developing a heart of gratitude. You may choose only to do one component of this exercise or all of them as needed.

ACTIVITY 1. STOP, LOOK, AND MOVE FORWARD

1. Take a few minutes right now to pause and consider what you're grateful for.
2. Look around, stay present, and identify what's good.
3. Pray and thank the Lord for anything that comes to mind or anything you see. It doesn't matter how big or small.
4. Move forward with an eternal focus, remembering that problems aren't so big in light of eternity. It helps keep them in perspective compared to the goodness of God and all he has given you to be grateful for.

1. List 3 to 10 things you are grateful for, using only one word at a time.
2. Give thanks to God as you thank him for everything you listed.

ACTIVITY 3. GRATITUDE PRAYER JOURNAL

1. Write a prayer from your heart about things you are grateful for.
2. Expand on this written prayer by telling God what it means to you to have those things. Stay focused only on what you're grateful for.

TIP

Keep a designated notebook for developing lists of things you're grateful for and your gratitude prayers so you can add to them daily or as often as you like.

Where Are You?

Learning how to be present in pain while sharing your
heart and giving your needs to the Lord.

10 minutes

In the Garden of Eden (Genesis 3), Adam and Eve felt immediate
shame when they ate the fruit from the tree that God told them not to
eat from. While they were hiding in nakedness and shame, they heard
God amongst them. The Lord called out to them and said, "Where are
you?" They responded that they were naked and afraid, so they hid.

Hiding, especially from God, can be a natural response, especially
when we carry shame or pain. In this exercise, you will deeply ponder
this three-word question, "Where are you?" Just as God knew exactly
where Adam and Eve were, he also knows where you are. He still asked
this question of Adam and Eve because he wanted to reconnect with
them and remind them that he was still there. It's a question meant to
bring back a relationship.

1. When you feel pain or sadness, or when your body is tense or
   hectic, imagine God asking you, "Where are you?"
2. Tap into some of the hard feelings you have. Pay attention to
   how your body is responding as well. Maybe your shoulders
   creep up to your ears, or you begin to fidget as you desire to
   run away.

3. When you think of God asking, "Where are you?" pause, look inward, and then respond by answering in three ways: Where am I physically? Where am I spiritually? Where am I emotionally?

   "Lord, I am in a place of physical tension. I am uptight and not relaxed. I can't seem to turn my mind off. I feel very far from you. I don't feel like I can hear you anymore. I am sad and frustrated."

4. After you identify your pain and give words to it by pouring your heart out to the Lord, invite him into it. Invite him to sit with you, and even when pain or anxiety is present, so is he.

······························· *TIP* ································

Make this exercise a daily habit. Use in times of stress, sadness, or anger to hear God asking, "Where are you?" and then tell him.

Write and Rip

Coming to terms with your feelings and letting go.

5 minutes

You may not always have the opportunity to fully express your mind. Sometimes, this is because you don't have access to talk to that person, and other times, it's because the things you want to say wouldn't be beneficial. When sharing isn't possible, it's important to have a place to process those words and allow your heart to share them.

In this write and rip exercise, you can do exactly that: share your words and let them go.

1. Write a letter to the person you need or want to speak to. Don't hold back. Don't worry about language or tone. Allow your heart to express everything freely.
2. Pause and ask the Lord to rid you of this grudge, the pain, and all the pent-up feelings and words you just wrote.
3. To symbolize letting go, rip up your letter and throw it away.

You can use this method of writing and ripping a letter anytime you have feelings or thoughts that deserve to be raw and unfiltered.

Gaining Hope and Confidence during Dark Times

············ USEFUL FOR ············

Gaining reassurance and building hope in the
middle of fear and difficult times.

············ TIME ············

15 to 20 minutes

············ INSTRUCTIONS ············

When life is hard and fears are prevalent, digging into Scripture to be reminded of God is one of the best and most comforting things you can do. Sitting in his presence and allowing his words to wash over you is something all of our hearts long for, especially when we're hurting or afraid.

In this exercise, dig into Psalm 46, remember who God is, and then have a time of reflection.

1. Slowly read each verse in each group.

    God: Our Source of Hope
    God is our refuge and strength, always ready to help in times of trouble. So we will not fear when earthquakes come and the mountains crumble into the sea. Let the oceans roar and foam. Let the mountains tremble as the waters surge! (v. 1–2)

    God's Presence: Our Reason for Hope
    A river brings joy to the city of our God, the sacred home of the Most High. God dwells in that city; it cannot be destroyed. From the very break of day, God will protect it. The nations are in chaos, and their kingdoms crumble! God's voice thunders,

and the earth melts. The Lord of Heaven's Armies is here among us; the God of Israel is our fortress. (v. 7–11)

God's Calling: To Experience His Presence

Come, see the glorious works of the Lord: See how he brings destruction upon the world. He causes wars to end throughout the earth. He breaks the bow and snaps the spear; he burns the shields with fire. "Be still, and know that I am God! I will be honored by every nation. I will be honored throughout the world. The Lord of Heaven's Armies is here among us; the God of Israel is our fortress." (v. 8–11)

2. Answer and reflect on each question.

   - Where are you tempted to cave into fear? Explain.
   - What does it mean to you that God is your refuge, strength, and fortress?
   - Has God ever sustained you before in your life? How could remembering that help you today?
   - How can the testimonies in the above verses give you hope for the situation you are dealing with today?
   - What would "Be still and know that I am God" look like in your life and situation today? Are you willing to do that?
   - God is asking you to trust him. Will you?

3. Pray and ask the Lord to remind you that he is in control. Surrender all your fears to him.

························· *TIP* ·························

Go deeper by choosing another Psalm to read today and see what else you can learn about who God is.

God's Truth

Anchoring your heart in the truth of God's Word and finding peace through being reminded of his character.

5 to 15 minutes

Scripture tells us that the Word of God is living and active and holds power to transform our lives. When we create space in our lives to get in the Word and truly get to know God personally through his Word, he can quickly become someone we trust, want to follow, and pursue a constant relationship with.

As you go through this exercise and look at each Scripture, ask yourself: "What does this verse tell me about God?" instead of "What does this verse have for me?" Focus on getting to know him. This is important because sometimes when we have pain in our lives, we tend to simply search for answers in the Bible. While this can be helpful, we look to Scripture to ultimately remind ourselves of who God is.

1. Pray and ask God to reveal himself to you as you read his Word.
2. Choose any number of verses you'd like to explore and read them one at a time.
3. On paper or in a journal, write what you learned about God from each verse listed below.

- Deuteronomy 7:9
- Psalm 66:19
- Psalm 116:1
- Isaiah 26:3-4

- Isaiah 41:13
- Isaiah 43:2
- 1 Corinthians 1:8-9
- 2 Corinthians 12:9-10
- 2 Thessalonians 1:6-7

················· *TIP* ·································

Take this activity one step further by writing out the entire Scripture and/or opting to memorize it.

Letter to Self

Taking a moment for reflection, finding healing, and gaining insight.

10 to 15 minutes

Writing a letter to your past, current, or future self can be healing. When you think without speaking or writing, you have about 1250 words a minute rolling around in your mind. This can often leave you reeling, ruminating, or falling into a downward spiral. However, when you speak, you greatly slow things down to around 125 words a minute, and it gets even slower when you write. This slowness allows more space in your mind to process thoughts, creativity to see new things, and a little room to breathe and calm down.

1. Choose who you will write this letter to: your past, current, or future self.
2. Pick a letter-writing prompt and begin to write.

- I would like to tell my younger self . . .
- To the future me, I would tell myself . . .
- I am proud of who I am now because . . .
- I forgive myself for . . .
- I know these things were not my fault because . . .
- I forgive myself for . . .
- I was too young to know better when I . . .

- I would tell myself to do (XYZ) differently.
- I will never do (XYZ) in the future.
- I think you should let go of . . .

As you finish your letter, close with any final thoughts you have or with whatever comes to mind. Ask God to guide you closer to his will.

·················· *TIP* ··································

While writing, you may find heavy emotions surfacing. If so, take some time to pause and complete **Where are You? exercise on page 134** before returning to finish this prompt.

Practicing Worship

Shifting your focus onto the Lord, developing a thankful heart, and winning battles over the attacks of the Enemy.

10 to 20 minutes

Choosing to worship during difficult times is a powerful way to recenter your mind on the heart of Christ. You can worship by reciting and claiming God's Word and through music. Many songs draw on Scripture for inspiration. And the Psalms were originally sung, so worship and music go hand in hand. As you complete this exercise, you can choose to do both or just one.

1. Recite each verse and offer up a prayer of praise and thanksgiving to the Lord for each one.

    - **Psalm 13:5-6:** But I trust in your unfailing love. I will rejoice because you have rescued me. I will sing to the Lord because he is good to me.
    - **Psalm 145:3:** Great is the Lord! He is most worthy of praise! No one can measure his greatness.
    - **Isaiah 25:1:** O Lord, I will honor and praise your name, for you are my God. You do such wonderful things! You planned them long ago, and now you have accomplished them.
    - **Romans 11:36:** For everything comes from him and exists by his power and is intended for his glory. All glory to him forever! Amen.

2. Choose a category and look up as you listen to each song, surrendering your heart to the Lord in worship.

For when I need forgiveness

- "Holy Water" by We the Kingdom
- "Forgiven" by David Crowder
- "Run to the Father" by Cody Carnes

For when I need to remember who God is

- "Good Good Father" by Chris Tomlin
- "Waymaker" by Leeland
- "Goodness of God" by CeCe Winans

For when I need encouragement

- "Heaven Stands Up" by Jared Anderson
- "I Surrender All" by CeCe Winans
- "O Come to the Altar" by Phil Wickham

For when I want to praise God

- "Holy Forever" by Chris Tomlin
- "In Christ Alone" by Shane & Shane

.... *TIP* ....

For an extended time of worship create a playlist on whatever platform you listen to music so you can listen to them at any time. Alternatively, participate in corporate worship at your church and open your heart to God through your praise.

Filling Your Joy Bucket

Lowering stress, making obstacles easier to handle
and overcome, and making joy a daily habit.

1 to 30 minutes

In all his creative brilliance, the Lord spared no attention to detail when he created our brains. The right orbital prefrontal cortex, also less formally known as the "joy bucket," is in the front of the brain. It's a portion of your brain designed to hold joy and rest. What's amazing about this joy bucket is that we are told more than five hundred times to practice joy in Scripture. God not only calls us to practice joy, but he also gives us a special place to contain it!

Think of joy as a gift you can choose to open every day. In this three-option exercise, examine the many ways to incorporate the gift of joy into your daily life. Rotate between these exercises or complete one category at a time. You may also decide to focus on one category per week. Reap the benefits of the good medicine of having a joyful heart (Proverbs 17:22).

1. Make a list of joy-filled activities to choose from. Create this list by determining things that you like to do. These are things that make you feel happy, rested, or energized. Make sure they take varied amounts of time so that you have a range of options.

2. Once the list is complete, choose one thing to make a daily habit or dedicate to doing it at least once a week. Add to this list as often as you'd like. Here are some examples:

- Go for a walk
- Listen to music
- Read
- Take a bath
- Spend time with a friend
- Cook a healthy meal

OPTION 2

1. Incorporate joy in your daily life by:

- Asking God to fill you with it every morning.
- Reading a verse about joy and meditating on it. For example:

  o Psalm 118:24
  o Proverbs 17:22
  o Philippians 4:4

2. Create a joy-filled mindset by getting up daily and saying, "Today, I will choose joy!"

OPTION 3

1. Remove anything that steals joy from your life. For example:

- Fear-based or stressful media or news.
- Toxic relationships.

- Social media that makes you feel envy, comparison, or stress.
- A job that drains you. Begin to make plans for a new career or job.

.... *TIP* ....

Research Scripture about joy, write the Scripture references, and try to commit to biblical joy by picking one to read every morning.

Visualizing God's Justice

Letting go of the burdens of the pain of injustice.

15 minutes

Amid the unfair and unjust trials of this world, one of the hopes we have is that the day of judgment will one day come. Until it does, we must find a way to live in peace without proper justice in our lifetime.

In this exercise, you will learn how to find comfort and hope in the justice of God instead of longing for it on this side of eternity.

1. Before you begin, find an appropriate time and quiet space where you can settle your heart and prepare yourself to pause and look inward. As you settle, ask yourself how you feel about any injustice being done. Pray and ask the Lord to meet your heart as you go through this exercise.

2. Romans 12:19 reminds us that retaliation is in the Lord's hands. As you sit before God close your eyes and think about the injustice that has taken place. Feel it in your hands. Grip them tight and hold on to every wrongdoing and unfair thing that has happened. Feel the weightiness of them.

3. Envision God's hand of justice swooping in. See how much bigger and more powerful he is. When you're ready, open your hands and give him all the injustice you've been carrying. Sit with your hands open in prayer to the Lord for however long you need.

4. As you've given him your burdens, recall seeing his open hands one more time. See his hands reaching for you, embracing you, reminding you that he is taking care of this on your behalf.

5. Picture yourself at a peaceful place now that the Lord has lifted your heavy burdens. Imagine yourself at the beach, staring into the ocean or gazing across a mountain range. In this moment, feel your shoulders drop, feel the lightness return to your open hands. See yourself getting up and moving forward that much lighter. Envision how freely you can move now without these burdens.

6. Give God praise for his justice and thank him that because of his Son, one day, all evil will be no more.

.... *TIP* ....

If going through all the steps feels too heavy, take your time. You may remain on one as long as you need to, or you can come back to any of them at a later time. There is no need to rush.

Making Time to Celebrate

Taking the time to celebrate wins and live the abundant life God calls us to.

10 minutes for the exercise, varied times to execute

John 10:10 tells us, "The thief's purpose is to steal and kill and destroy. My purpose is to give them a rich and satisfying life." A broken heart can become something the enemy can use in your life to steal your peace and hope. He longs to steal from you mentally, emotionally, physically, and spiritually. And he will steal as much and as often as he can get away with. God, on the other hand, wants to add to your life. He wants your life to have abundant goodness.

This exercise is all about celebrating your wins and the freedom forgiveness gives you. Since you'll soon be out of a hard season or are there already, it's time for abundant fun and rest.

1. Take time to write out a list of fun things for you or things you want to try one day. That's it. Don't think about if they're possible or if you'd be good at them, only think about things you would like.

2. You may write one long list or divide your list into two catego-ries, "What's Fun" and "What I'd Like to Try."

Examples:

What's Fun

- Hiking
- Going on a picnic
- Riding my bike
- Singing

What I'd Like to Try

- Take a cooking class
- Learn to make pottery
- Play on a recreational sports league
- Skydiving

3. Once you have your list, start choosing one thing to do a week or, depending on how extensive and available it is to you, once a month.

.... *TIP* ....

Keep your list visible so you can be reminded of it often. If you're not ready to celebrate the win of forgiveness yet, keep adding to this list.

Motivation Chart

Evaluating and discerning the benefits of change. Assessing the disadvantages of remaining the same.

20 minutes

We rarely make decisions without a reason. Your motivation to do something may arise from something you've done in the past that worked, or just the opposite. Maybe you got hurt the last time you did it, so now you're much more unlikely to make the same choice again.

When someone has betrayed your trust, and you're deciding whether to take a leap of faith again, or whether or not forgiving someone will be worth it, sometimes the most helpful thing you can do is take a step back and look at the bigger picture.

As you move through this motivation chart step by step, you can gain some clarity over your next step.

1. Draw a large, evenly divided four-quadrant square with enough room to write in each box on a sheet of paper.

2. Title each square with these four titles:

Reasons to Stay the Same	Reasons to Face My Fears
What the Future Holds for Me if Things Stay the Same	What the Future Holds for Me if I Face My Fears

3. Fill in each box with as many details as possible as you think of your situation and any decisions you must make. You may not have the exact answer but take the time to ponder and determine the most likely outcome.

4. Evaluate your answers and determine which response will more likely get you closest to where you'd like to be next.

.... *TIP* ....

Invite God into your evaluation and decision-making process. Pause to pray at each step and ask him to help guide you into clarity.

Exploring Forgiveness

Uncovering your personal beliefs and feelings on forgiveness, as you begin to process and move forward.

20 minutes

This exercise aims to break forgiveness down into smaller steps to help deconstruct what may appear like a daunting process. Examine your beliefs about forgiveness and make space for your thoughts and feelings while ultimately asking the Lord to speak truth over you.

No matter how small, every step forward in understanding forgiveness and walking toward it is healthy progress—you are following the Lord's call to become a good forgiver.

1. Look at the list below and choose two words that most reflect your thoughts on forgiveness. Write them down on a separate piece of paper.

    - Forgetting
    - Pardoning
    - Excusing
    - Reconciling
    - Condoning
    - Accepting
    - Letting Go
    - Moving On

2. As you reflect on the words you chose, ask yourself the questions below. Write down your answers.

- Why do I believe those words are connected to forgiveness?
- How do those words make me feel? Do they stir up bitterness, anger, fear, etc.?
- Where do I get that belief system on forgiveness? Have the examples of forgiveness I've seen shaped my beliefs? Have the times I've been wronged by others influenced what I believe about forgiveness?
- What does it mean if I were to (fill in a word from the above list in the present tense), i.e., forget, accept, let go? Does your answer make you feel better or worse?
- Is it possible that your beliefs about forgiveness have blocked your ability to forgive or made it more difficult?

3. What insights did you gain?
4. Ask God to reveal anything to you that he wants you to know.

·············· *TIP* ··············

Expand on this exercise by reviewing each word on the list and evaluating it, or adding a word to the list that isn't on it. Always remember to ask God if what you believe is true.

Steps to Asking for Forgiveness

Offering up a genuine apology that helps with reconciliation.

15 minutes for the exercise, varied times to execute

As believers, we are called to be ministers of reconciliation, just as Jesus is (2 Corinthians 5:18,20). With such a high calling, we aren't let off the hook when it comes to apologizing and making efforts to restore broken relationships. We are also called to live at peace with everyone as much as it is up to us (Romans 12:18). Essentially, we have been given three jobs in these Scriptures: to own our sin, seek forgiveness, and do our part in living in peace with others.

When we have wronged someone and are seeking forgiveness, there are necessary components of an apology that must be present for it to be genuine and received as well as possible. In this exercise, we will go through each component step by step to prepare you to present an authentic apology or request for forgiveness.

If you need God's forgiveness, start with the first segment before moving on to the next. In the second segment, go through each step and think about your answers. Write them down if that will be helpful to you.

God has already initiated the forgiveness process. Your part is obedience to accept the gift he has offered. Here's how:

- Repent. Seek forgiveness to repair your relationship with him by repenting of the specific sins that led you astray or made you disobedient to the life he has called you to live. Admit to the Lord that you understand that you are a sinner who has fallen short of the glory of God, just as all of us have (Romans 3:23).
- Believe and receive the forgiveness that God has offered to you.
- Move forward with a surrendered heart that desires to follow the Lord's will and his instruction for your life.

STEPS TO RECEIVING FORGIVENESS

1. Read Psalm 32:1-5 and then start with prayer, asking the Lord to reveal everything you have done wrong.
2. Verbally apologize and acknowledge that you hurt the person you're apologizing to.

   I'm sorry that I hurt you.

3. Take ownership of what you did without making excuses.

   I'm sorry I raised my voice and spoke to you in a belittling tone.

4. Be willing to receive any feedback or thoughts they share with you without getting defensive. Keep your humble spirit engaged.

   I hear you and understand how that may have made you feel dismissed.

5. Share any steps you are taking to make sure the same offense won't happen again.

   The next time I feel myself getting frustrated, instead of lashing out, I will let you know I need a minute to calm down.

6. If the situation requires it, offer any repair.

   I am sorry my not paying attention to the time made me late for us to go on our date. I will call and arrange a sitter and take you out tomorrow.

7. Request forgiveness and allow them to answer honestly without forcing them to forgive you. Be willing to be patient.

   Will you please forgive me? However, I understand if you need more time to process what happened.

8. If given the opportunity, begin to rebuild trust.

········· *TIP* ·········

When voicing an apology, observe your tone and body language. They are just as important as your words. Make sure your heart is in a place of repentance before you seek forgiveness from God or anyone else.

Identifying an Ideal Friend

Discerning how to find someone trustworthy to come alongside you in support to make challenging times easier.

15 minutes

Friendships are important and add richness to our lives. It's important to share your story with the right kind of friend when you're looking to lean on someone and fully trust them to have a voice in your life. It's even more important that you don't allow a friend to replace the Lord. He will always be your first and only perfect friend.

By learning what Scripture says makes a good friend, you can evaluate your current friendships and invest in the connections that are worth trusting and confiding in. You will also brainstorm some attributes that are important for *you* in your ideal friend. Finally, you will learn how to *be* a good friend to someone else.

1. Read the Scriptures below about good traits in a friend.
2. Think of your friends and see how they reflect each trait according to Scripture.

- Proverbs 18:24—A good friend "sticks closer than a brother" and stands by you.
- Proverbs 27:17—A good friendship is one where "iron sharpens iron," and you make one another better.
- John 15:13—A good friend "lays down their life" and makes sacrifices for you.

- Proverbs 17:17—A good friend "is always loyal."
- 1 Thessalonians 5:11—A good friend "encourages" you.

3. Answer the questions below to identify an ideal friend.

- What trait is most important to me in a good friend?
- How do I like to be supported by a friend?
- How available do I need a friend to be?
- How important is it that they share their burdens with me, too?
- What would I consider to be red flags that I should avoid?
- Do I know anyone who would be my ideal friend, or do I need to try to develop a deeper friendship with a current friend?

4. Identify one or more friends you would be willing to trust or be open to make new connections with and/or friends that may fit your profile.

·· *TIP* ································

The Bible has a lot to say about friendships. If you want to dig deeper, do a search on friendship in the Bible and you'll find better traits to look for.

Wake Up Your Self-Worth

Creating a foundation of truth and positivity at the start of the day.

TIME

5 minutes

INSTRUCTIONS

Your daily habits reflect how emotionally, mentally, and physically healthy your life is. Your habits are even more powerful when they are rooted in the truth of God's Word. Many people wake up in the morning after hitting the snooze button a few times, roll over, and immediately check their phones, inviting stress into their lives without even thinking. They will bombard themselves with the messages found in social media or their inbox instead of the message of Scripture.

It's important to start your day with life-giving and productive habits to help you launch into your day on the right foot. How you view yourself and what you claim as your identity matters. A healthy and godly self-image helps you set boundaries, make good choices, continue on the journey of forgiveness, and decreases the likelihood that others will chip away at your self-worth.

Follow these exercises to start your day:

1. Instead of checking your phone first thing in the morning, sit up, ground your feet on the floor, and wake up your nervous system by gently tapping different parts of your body, starting with your head down to your toes.

2. Stand in front of the mirror and choose one identity-based Scripture to claim each morning or focus on the same one for a week.

- Genesis 1:27—"I am made in the image of God!"
- Psalm 139:14—"I am fearfully and wonderfully made!"
- Luke 6:27—"I can love my enemies as Christ calls me to!"
- 2 Corinthians 5:17—"I am a new creation!"
- Ephesians 2:10—"I am his masterpiece!"
- Colossians 3:13—"I am forgiven by God and will forgive others!"
- 1 Peter 2:9—"I am chosen!"

3. Release some dopamine by looking at yourself in the mirror and giving yourself a high five as you head into your day.

·· *TIP* ··

Simplify this exercise by writing verses on sticky notes to be readily available to read on your bathroom mirror. You may also alternate weekly between reading Scripture and playing worship songs.

Attributes of God

Getting to know and trust God more.

5 to 15 minutes

It's hard to follow what God says about forgiveness if we don't fully trust him. And that trust can only come from knowing him and spending time with him.

Familiarize yourself with who God is and learn about his character and heart as you examine God's attributes in this exercise. Spend time looking up each verse and continuously ask him to reveal himself. Share your desire to know him more.

1. Pray first. Let God know you want to know him more. Invite him to point you to the trait he wants you to understand about him today.

2. Select one or more attributes from the list and look up each verse it is taken from.

Attributes

- Patient—2 Peter 3:9
- All-Powerful—Psalm 147:5
- Righteous—Psalm 119:137
- Eternal—Isaiah 40:28
- Loving and compassionate—Isaiah 30:18
- Merciful—Titus 3:5
- Wise—Isaiah 55:9

- Loving—1 John 4:16
- Holy—1 Peter 1:16
- Faithful—Hebrews 10:23
- Good—Psalm 100:5
- Unchanging—Malachi 3:6

3. Answer the questions for each attribute. You may ponder your answers or write them out.

- How does this trait help me trust God more?
- When have I experienced this trait of God in my own life?
- Does this verse help me forgive more easily? Why or why not?
- Do I struggle to believe this trait about God? Why or why not?

························· *TIP* ·······························

Complete this exercise in a notebook so that you can add more of his attributes and reflect on them when you need to remember who God is.

Evaluating Healthy Boundaries

Reflecting on your relationships and determining
if they are safe and healthy.

20 to 30 minutes

Many people believe boundaries are something you place on others. However, boundaries are something you place around yourself. They let others know what is okay with you and what isn't. People still have complete freedom with their choices and behaviors, but you get to maintain the power to decide whether you are willing to tolerate those choices and behaviors.

Setting boundaries is the best way to maintain relational health and your own emotional health. They are essential for creating and living a more toxic-free life. As you go through this exercise, you can use a journal to write your answers, discuss them with a trusted loved one, or reflect on them yourself. If you have multiple relationships or circumstances that need to be evaluated, go through the questions for each one individually, and then determine if any steps from the "How to Develop Boundaries" section are needed.

REFLECT AND ANSWER

1. What about this relationship or situation is not okay with me? What have I been or am I currently tolerating that I don't like?
2. Can I share how I feel safely and freely without being judged or shamed?

3. Is this a problem that continues to happen?
4. Have I seen any changed behavior, or has any trust been rebuilt?
5. If this relationship or situation remains the same, will that be okay with me?
6. How will I feel if I allow this relationship or situation to continue?

······················· *HOW TO DEVELOP BOUNDARIES* ·······················

1. Establish an appropriate time and share your expectations, what you need, or what you would like this person to stop or start doing. Focus on using "I" statements and stating your needs, not on blaming the other person. Avoid using "always" or "never." For example: "I want to keep having this conversation with you, but I need for you to lower your voice."
2. If the boundary is violated, speak up, tell the person their behavior is unacceptable, and share an appropriate consequence. For example: "If you continue to raise your voice at me, I won't keep talking with you."
3. Ensure the consequence happens if the boundary is disrespected.
4. If there is a lack of changed behavior after a violated boundary and consequence, it may be time to withdraw from or end this relationship.

································ *TIP* ································

Remember that sometimes, if the behavior is harmful or too hurtful, it is okay to skip all the steps and immediately withdraw from the relationship for emotional or physical safety.

How to Stop Ruminating

··········· *USEFUL FOR* ···········

Interrupting the rumination of negative thoughts
and replacing them with truth or acceptance.

··········· *TIME* ···········

5 to 20 minutes

··········· *INSTRUCTIONS* ···········

Whether you're dwelling on a decision, a painful event, or negative thoughts, ruminating or playing them over and over in your mind will keep you stuck or send you spiraling into stress and anxiety. In 2 Corinthians 10:5, the Apostle Paul tells us to "capture . . . rebellious thoughts and teach them to obey Christ." In other words, if our thoughts aren't good or godly, we must flip them on their heads!

If you are trying to make a decision that has your mind reeling in worry, or if you're caught in a negative thought cycle that is breeding fear or anxiety, going through these specific steps will help settle your mind and heart. These could be negative thoughts or fears about yourself, others, or a situation.

1. Create awareness around your negative thought patterns. Take notice when anxiety or worry arises. Anytime you feel your body physically respond to stress, ask yourself what you are thinking about. When you're not in a stressful moment, pause and reflect on any negative thoughts that consistently cause a stressful reaction.

    Anytime I think about my ex-friend, my stomach gets knots, and my chest tightens.

2. Identify your negative thoughts. Say them aloud.

   I will never get over what they did to me! I'm such a fool for trusting them!

3. Validate and allow your feelings to flow and then question if they are based on truth.

   I am scared I will never get over what's been done to me, but is this really true?

4. Challenge any lies with truth.

   I am scared that I will never recover from the pain it caused, but what is true is that God can heal my heart and mind.

5. Ask God to help you allow your feelings without believing any unhelpful lies.

   I feel scared, Lord. Help me believe you are with me and heal me.

6. Exchange your negative thoughts for truth.

   God can help me heal.

7. Relax and close your eyes. Visualize placing your negative thoughts on a leaf that you put in a stream or a balloon you're letting drift away. Follow it until it disappears.

8. Thank God for his truth.

·· *TIP* ····································

If you are unsure if your thoughts are truthful, search an online Bible for topics about your concerns and look for clarifying Scripture, or seek wisdom from a friend.

LEARNING HOW TO FORGIVE

Reframing Conflict

Transforming conflict from something negative
into a necessary part of finding solutions.

15 minutes

For some of us, conflict can mean chaos, yelling, and a break in relationships, thus making it something to avoid or fear. However, conflict is a natural part of life and relationships—it is a means to a solution-focused end. It is also a healthy way that two or more individuals can have differing thoughts and opinions.

Moving through this exercise, you will uncover your personal beliefs about conflict and how they were shaped. Observe a healthy perspective on conflict, where you can address problems or issues without fear or avoidance.

1. Do you see conflict as something negative or positive? Why? What examples of conflict have you seen that helped shape your views?
2. If you avoid conflict or dismiss poor behavior from others in your current situation, what will the end result look like?
3. What does healthy conflict look like to you? What potential good could come to your situation if you could have healthy conflict?
4. Is there anything you are afraid of happening in this situation? Are there other worries bothering you?

1. Enter conflict from a place of calm, where you can be open-minded.

2. Be prepared to listen to gain an understanding of another's perspective.

3. Keep the conversation in the present. Bring it back to the current time if it veers into the past or future.

4. Be mindful of your tone and be willing to ask the other person to address theirs as well.

5. Take personal responsibility for your part. Avoid taking responsibility for theirs.

6. Focus only on what you can control. Don't get roped into problems you can't do anything about.

TIP

If the person you are most concerned about having conflict with is potentially toxic, reference the **Evaluating Healthy Boundaries exercise on page 165.**

Practicing Acceptance

Learning how to let go of difficult emotions.

5 to 15 minutes

Difficult situations and emotions are inescapable parts of the forgiveness journey. Rather than stewing on them and allowing a negative mood or mindset, it's best to learn how to accept them as a reality. Acceptance does not make a situation acceptable. Rather, acceptance prevents it from continuing to affect you or your life negatively.

If you want to accept the things that you have no power or control to change, you will have to make acceptance a practice.

1. Acknowledge your pain, resistance, or feelings around the wrong that has been done or the challenging situation. You may want to make a bullet point list of every feeling you have toward the situation or the person who has inflicted it on you. To move forward, you will want to know exactly what you are letting go of.
2. Determine what holding on to those negative feelings or the pain of an unchanging situation has cost you. What have you lost by harboring those feelings?
3. Are you tired of having your life negatively impacted by these things or this person? Do you have any anger to release? Ask the Lord to help you let them go. It's okay to tell him you are tired and no longer wish to carry these burdens any longer.

4. Sit quietly and reflect with the Lord. Visualize surrendering these feelings, problems, or this person into his hands. Remain quiet until you feel his peace.
5. Move forward, treating yourself gently. It is hard to let go of things that have hurt you. If it is helpful, speak to yourself as if you were a child, asking for help. Remind yourself this is hard work and give yourself grace.
6. Practice throughout the day when those original feelings return.

TIP

Acceptance is heavy work. Doing this exercise outside in nature, on a walk, or in your favorite location that brings you peace may be beneficial.

ACKNOWLEDGMENTS

Without God's grace and forgiveness, this book would have never been possible for us to write. His great forgiveness of our sins has taught us to, sometimes painstakingly, learn to offer it to others freely. He gently reminds us of our own need for forgiveness during the times we have struggled to offer forgiveness to others. He has graciously redeemed every area of our lives that we thought was stolen by the pain of our individual stories and struggles.

Thank you also to our family for the constant joy you bring us and the support you each offer, especially during those approaching milestone deadlines. Thank you for always being willing to forgive us for our shortcomings as parents and as people. Your extended grace is a gift to our souls.

Thank you to the entire Zeitgeist team, who is always supportive and encouraging and brings out the best in our writing abilities. You truly are a dream team!

Lastly, thank you to everyone who has caused us harm intentionally or unintentionally. You have taught us to turn to the Lord and model our lives after him. You have allowed us to experience beauty from the ashes, and for that, we are grateful.

ABOUT THE
AUTHORS

Chris and Jamie Bailey are professional Christian counselors and marriage coaches. They have been married for over 30 years and, together, raised three daughters and have four wonderful grand-children. They run a private practice in South Carolina as well as *Expedition Marriage*, a global online marriage ministry. Their passion is sharing the hope and truth of Jesus with couples through speaking, writing, running marriage retreats, creating online courses, and as hosts of the *Expedition Marriage* podcast. They desire to help couples and individuals break free from anything that keeps them in captivity so they can live an abundant life through Jesus. Learn more and access their online resources at expeditionmarriage.org.

Hi there,

We hope you found *Learning How to Forgive* helpful. If you have any questions or concerns about your book, or have received a damaged copy, please contact customerservice@penguinrandomhouse.com. We're here and happy to help.

Also, please consider writing a review on your favorite retailer's website to let others know what you thought of the book.

Sincerely,

The Zeitgeist Team